TUMANOV

TUMANOV

Confessions of a KGB Agent

Oleg Tumanov

Translated by David Floyd

edition q, inc
Chicago, Berlin, Tokyo, and Moscow

©1993 by edition q, inc., Carol Stream, Illinois.

Also available in German as *Gest ä ndnisse eines KGB-Agenten*, by edition q Verlags-GmbH, Berlin, Germany.

Library of Congress Cataloging-in-Publication Data

Tumanov, Oleg.
    Tumanov : confessions of a KGB agent / Oleg Tumanov ; translated by David
    Floyd.
        p.   cm.
    Translated from an unpublished manuscript.
    Also published in German under title: Gest ä ndnisse eines KGB — Agenten.
    ISBN 0-86715-269-9
    1. Soviet Union.   Komitet gosudarstvennoĭ bezopastnosti.   2. Tumanov,
Oleg.   3. Intelligence officers — Soviet Union — Biography.   I. Title.   II. Title:
Confessions of a KGB agent.
    HV8224.T928   1993
    363.2'83'092 — dc20
    [B]   93-6427
                                                                                                    CIP

Manufactured in the United States of America

Contents

Part III   Return to Moscow

Foreword

This is the story of a spy, an imposter—not exactly a dream job, whether one is paid in rubles, dollars, shekels, or Marks. The appraisal of a secret agent's accomplishments depends on the point of view of the appraiser; often celebrated as a hero by those who employ him, he is to his victims a contemptuous creature who should be put in prison. A spy's personality is, of necessity, as split as the reaction to his work, the split widening in proportion to the length of his double life. He is caught in the vise of two identities, he serves as he betrays. The fact is that, in terms of ideology and character, the borders between truth, reality, and illusion are blurred among even the most well-established members of this ancient profession. The wary glance over the shoulder, the never-relenting fear of discovery, of being exposed, the pressure of giving a perfect performance twenty-four hours a day, three hundred and sixty-five days a year merely to survive, of assuming a mask that becomes a second skin—all of these automatically alter the psyche of the foreign agent over time.

This is not, however, the report of a traitor, a defector. To Oleg Tumanov, the Soviet Union was "the greatest country in the world," and even today he prefers Russia to Germany or America or the West. That was and remains his right. Oleg Tumanov is convinced that he fought on the right side during the Cold War, and this conviction must be granted him. He did not have to follow the orders of the KGB to return to Moscow after his work was accomplished; he could have continued his quite pleasant life as director of the American-sponsored Radio Liberty, with the "West's blessing." Nor did he trim his sails to the wind when the Russian people toppled the detested monument located in the front of his feared headquarters, destroying the foundations of both his state and his beliefs. Oleg Tumanov, although living in retirement on the pension of a colonel, is still a member of the KGB. And that is something that the reader must keep in mind.

The KGB is not some chaotic, leaderless, and defenseless discount warehouse in Moscow that is putting up for grabs secret files and background information to the hordes of foreign publishers and journalists who are rushing in, hard cash in hand. Nothing comes out of the cellars and vaults of the fortress of the Lubyanka that the KGB does not wish to have released. This was a lesson Boris Yeltsin was to learn when he decreed that all state archives be opened to and put at the disposal of an agency of his own creation; a decree coolly shelved by the KGB.

Formally speaking, the KGB no longer exists now that it is legally part of the Ministry of Security and Directorate for External Intelligence. But its infrastructure remains intact, both internally and internationally, and to a certain extent it is more powerful today even than in the time of Joseph Stalin. When the dictator in the Kremlin demanded the head of the KGB it seldom took more than a week before a report of execution was delivered. Should Yeltsin express a similar wish today, there would probably be not one, but several, casualties—those who had died laughing. And this is also something the reader should keep in mind while reading Oleg Tumanov's report.

There are those observers and insiders of the scene who are convinced that Tumanov is not the author, or not the sole author, of his memoirs; that the KGB was guiding his hand. Leonid Finkelstein, Tumanov's disillusioned colleague and onetime superior at Radio Liberty, numbers among these skeptics. To him, his old pal Tumanov is a "mouthpiece" misused by the KGB, and a willing instrument of its continuing campaign of disinformation. I myself know that Vladimir Snegirev, the well-known Moscow journalist, assisted the author in the writing of this book. Snegirev owes this job not to the KBG, however, but to representatives of my publishing house, edition q, in Russia's capital city. It may be assumed that before Tumanov delivered his manuscript it was gone over, word-by-word, line-by-line, and, when deemed necessary, edited by the ever image-conscious and information-hungry Ministry of Security. To my question of whether he had the approval of his old employer, Oleg Tumanov answered, "They have no objections to my book in its present form." The reader should keep this in mind as well.

Leonid Finkelstein is also convinced that Tumanov was a true and credible dissident when, as a sailor, he jumped over the side of his Soviet ship and swam to freedom. He believes it was only later, probably in 1971, when Tumanov was already working for Radio Liberty and a student at the University of Glasgow, that he signed on with the KGB. (Tumanov, incidentally, does not mention this year in Scotland in his memoirs. Perhaps this is due to the fact that, according to the university's records, he did not pass any of his course examinations in Soviet Literature, or in the History of the USSR and the Revolutionary Process. It has been established that the "student" was frequently absent for long periods of time, on holiday in Spain or, more likely, in East Berlin or Moscow, where he was pursuing his true interests.)

Finkelstein's misgivings correspond to the CIA's official version of the story. The agency questions Tumanov's account of the way in which he was recruited in Moscow, with the comment that it fully contradicts all known KGB methods and practices. Colonel Oleg Nechiporenko, whom John Barron, author of the standard work, *Inside the KGB*, calls one of the organization's most brilliant minds, and who discovered, recruited, and later guided the young Komsomol (Soviet youth organization) activist Tumanov as operations commander, fully understands the CIA's interpretation of Tumanov's escape that has been put forward by this old counterparts in Langley, Virginia: "Following Oleg's return in 1986, the Americans were left standing there looking foolish and embarrassed. Tumanov had slipped through their system. They had interrogated him for weeks, for months, had hooked him up to a lie detector several times and filled out a certificate of non-objection on him. Washington probably asked the CIA a number of uncomfortable questions after that.

"The determination that Tumanov was 'clean' when he was put through the wringer, and only later, under pressure, began to work as an informant for the KGB, can be seen as a plausible explanation. But this theory totally ignores the facts. The agent business is not determined by logic and routine; on the contrary, the use of applied logic and continuity of method and operation is dangerous. We have found our collaborators in distinctly different ways. Panning first this way, then that, Tumanov was one of the gold pieces we filtered out. That we were correct in not initiating Oleg into, or schooling him in, the details of his mission before it began, in never, for example, taking him to KGB headquarters during that time, is supported by the fact that the CIA found nothing. Had Oleg been burdened by too much knowledge, it is possible he would not have passed the lie detector tests."

Tumanov himself calls attention to another weak link in the CIA's argument; namely, the assertion that in Glasgow the KGB had applied the old familiar thumbscrew of ". . . or your family in Moscow will have difficulties." His answer to this: "My mother, my father, and my uncle were officers in the KGB, in part even attained the rank of general. Subject closed?"

We would of course, have preferred to hear more concrete details from our author on his actual work for Radio Liberty. I myself questioned him closely about this in Moscow over the Easter holidays in 1993. Why I experienced only limited success was explained to me by retired Colonel Oleg Nechiporenko: "Your expectation that Tumanov provide you with complete and detailed information on his activities betrays a certain naïvete on your part. Oleg was a link, a part of an operation. An important link, it is true, but only that. And this operation isn't completed. The fact that Radio Liberty now has an office in Moscow doesn't change the basic situation. Had Tumanov reported to you in detail exactly what his duties were, then the CIA would know what the KGB was doing there, today and tomorrow. The KGB is not dead."

And that is something that not just readers alone should take to heart.

—HENNO LOHMEYER

Part I

We Have Other Plans for You

A Box of Matches

November 1969. Friday. The City of Munich. As was my custom, I was eating my evening meal in a cozy little Yugoslav restaurant, which was about a ten-minute walk from my apartment. I had settled down at my favorite table and ordered a meat dish with spicy sauce, some red wine, and a glass of *slivovice.* The restaurant's plum brandy was especially good: it was homemade and kept for regular customers. The owner of the restaurant gave me a welcoming smile from behind the bar—she was long used to serving the young Russian émigré who often dropped in for his evening meal and to leaf through the evening papers over coffee.

As usual, there were few other customers. An elderly Bavarian couple at the other end of the little restaurant was just finishing their meal, and a man with curly hair, wearing a tweed jacket, was sitting at the door passing the time over a mug of beer. It seemed to me that I had seen him there the last time I had dropped in. On that occasion as well, he had been sitting with his back to the window, studying the beer in his mug. On this occasion our eyes met for a moment and I had the impression that I knew him and that he knew me. But he gave no sign of recognition and continued studying the froth on his beer.

"That's odd," I thought to myself. "We have certainly met somewhere before. But where?"

The owner took curly-hair's money and disappeared into the kitchen. The stranger then rose from his table, apparently intending to leave. But first he began searching his pockets for matches to light his cigarette— only to find he had none. So he approached me and asked—in bad German—whether I could give him a light. Our eyes met again as I handed him a box of matches. He gave me a scarcely noticeable nod. I would remember who he was in a moment. Calmly he lit his cigarette and put the box of matches down on the table. But it was not my box he put down, but a quite different one, of the kind you find lying around in hotels and restaurants. "Danke schön," he said and then turned on his heel and made for the door. He departed and we never met again.

It was then that I recalled where we had met before: it had been in Moscow, five or six years before, when, as a member of the Communist youth organization, I had taken part in campaigns organized by the KGB to rid the city of illegal traders and currency dealers. The curly-headed stranger had been the leader of our group, which had been given the job of "cleansing" the hotels used by foreign tourists.

I picked up the matchbox the man had left behind. There was nothing special about it—on the outside was the usual advertisement for some drinks manufactured in West Berlin. Below that, however, on a plain background, were two dates carefully written with a ballpoint pen. My heart skipped a beat. It meant that the day had come: the matchbox told me when and where the long-awaited meeting would take place.

I quickly paid my bill and set off for home. I needed to be alone to weigh the situation and to think. My life was about to take a sharp turn. It had been a long time since I had felt as I did at that moment, clutching the colored matchbox in my hand. Those matches could well light the fuse of a mine that could explode and blow me to pieces.

It had been just four years since I had successfully staged an escape from the Soviet Union. The task with which the KGB had entrusted me consisted of infiltrating myself into the company of Russian émigrés, establishing my position among them, and then trying to expose the links between the émigrés and the American secret services. "But the most important thing is simply to get yourself firmly established in any Western country"—those were the instructions given to me by the KGB officers—"Put down some roots, provide yourself with connections and a job. Only then should you make use of our agreed upon signal. That will enable us to find you." It might not be soon, they warned me in Moscow. "And it is possible that you will seem to have been forgotten and crossed off the record. But never fear, when you are needed, we will be in touch with you. Remember, the first person to make contact with you will be someone known to you. For the rest, don't worry your head about anything."

I didn't worry. I had been so conscientiously carrying out my instructions to penetrate the society in which I found myself that I had long since made myself completely at home in the West. My relations in émigré circles could not have worked out better. I had good relations with the NIS, a Russian anti-Soviet organization, and I was working for Radio Liberty, which was funded by the CIA and broadcast the views of the émigrés to the Soviet Union. I had a blameless reputation and excellent prospects for advancement. The radio station provided me with a rent-free, fully furnished apartment in a new building and paid me a decent salary as well. I was able to travel around the world. I had acquired many interesting friends. And, I had adopted the Western way of life.

But now Moscow had decided that the moment had come for me to be reminded that I was first of all a spy, and that all the rest was secondary. This was a serious test for a man who was still only twenty-five years old.

So the time had come for the people in Moscow to remember that I existed and to involve me in active espionage. It meant goodbye to the unexciting life of a successful émigré. The KGB had kept its word: after four years they had tracked me down in Munich and the first contact had been made by someone I had met in the past. Everything was as they had promised. But what next?

As I walked past the brightly lit windows of Radio Liberty on Arabella Street I involuntarily slowed my pace. Only that morning I had entered the building as one of the many hundreds of people employed there. Tomorrow I should be "exposed" as an agent of the KGB.

It was the beginning of life with a "false bottom."

The two dates inscribed on the matchbox referred to two Sundays a week apart. I flew to Berlin on the morning of the first date. The Friedrichstrasse, the restaurant where the matchbox had come from, turned out to be situated next to Tempelhof Airport. I fixed myself up in a cheap rooming house, left my suitcase there and set out for a stroll around the city, which I was visiting for the first time. Toward lunchtime, I returned to the Friedrichstrasse.

The place where I ate my lunch was not really a restaurant, but a little bar that offered a choice of dishes commonly found in such a place: sausages with sauerkraut, goulash, pea soup, beer, and cheap schnapps. Nobody paid much attention to what others were doing. Customers sat down briefly to satisfy their appetites and then quickly left so that others could take their places. To pass the time, I ate some sausages and slowly drank a mug of beer. No one approached me or showed the slightest interest in me. I could hardly remain sitting there, so I resolved to try again that evening.

On the way back to my lodging I stopped by a newsstand and, while pretending to study the papers, looked around. I saw nothing suspicious. If someone was following me he was doing it very skillfully.

I bought the Berlin papers and a bottle of whisky. Back at my lodging I drank some of the whisky straight from the bottle to ease the tension. The whisky had little effect: the feeling of alarm I was experiencing would not go away.

As usual in such situations, time passed very slowly. First I tried to read, then I switched on the television, but nothing would rid me of my anxiety.

Maintaining contact is the most dangerous part of spying. Every operation is exposed to a double risk: each of the participants in a secret meeting may be "tailed" and so wreck the whole affair. The Americans had kept me under observation for a long time, but had stopped watching me about three years back. Since then I had not noticed that I was being followed or that counterintelligence was paying me any special attention. But what about this new partner from the KGB? Can one ever be one hundred percent sure? What if he was being followed?

In the evening I again sat at the bare wooden table in the little café on the Friedrichstrasse. I ordered a beer and looked around. Imagine my surprise when I saw my friend Sergei sitting in a corner, staring straight at me. Well, maybe "friend" is too strong a word—better call him my instructor in the KGB. He was the last person *over there* with whom I had contact before my departure for the West. He was the one who had assured me that sooner or later the KGB would find where I was and make contact. Apparently he had come himself.

I must have looked rather silly, because Sergei was unable to suppress the rather broad, self-satisfied grin across his face, and was not even trying to disguise it in any way. After a while he stood up and made his way to the toilet with an anxious look on his face. I followed him, as though hypnotized. There was nobody else in the toilet. We stood side by side and Sergei whispered: "Now follow me. Keep your distance, but don't let me out of your sight."

We went down a long empty street, lit by a few streetlamps. I just caught sight of a plainly dressed man, apparently a workman, who slipped in behind me: probably a colleague of Sergei's taking care of my rear. We turned onto a side street and proceeded to the entrance of a very old house where it was very dark. The "workman" left us, singing a tune to himself. Then Sergei embraced me, saying: "Greetings, Oleg! How are you? You've done well!"

In a couple of minutes he managed to instruct me about our next meeting. "In January you will take a week's leave and come to the same restaurant. You will see me, either at lunch or dinner, and we will go off together to East Berlin." He gave me a fresh box of matches with the dates of our next meetings and then vanished into the winter twilight. The "workman" followed me at a distance back to my lodging.

I had no difficulty taking ten days off work in January. On the second Sunday in 1970, I threw a track suit, a couple of shirts, and a razor into a rucksack and flew to Tempelhof on the same morning flight I had taken before. Sergei was expecting me at the café at midday. For about an hour and a half we strolled around at a good distance from each other, went to a few stations on the Metro, and visited a graveyard. Finally, when he was quite convinced that we were not being followed, we returned to the Friedrichstrasse, where there was an underground passage from West to East Berlin. We went down into the passage, but before we reached the crowd of people applying for visas to cross the border, Sergei directed me to a hardly noticeable side door. He showed the security officer his papers and, without a word, we were let through another door and out into the territory of the German Democratic Republic—East Germany.

I was struck by the rundown, gray appearance of Communist Berlin. The contrast with the West was very striking. In no more than a minute I had left the world of glittering shop windows, lively, open faces, beautiful cars, and well-maintained buildings for the grim world of "real socialism." One had the impression that in the East the war had only just ended and the camouflage had not yet been removed.

We got into a Volkswagen parked at the subway entrance, and only then did we allow our emotions to have their way: we embraced each other and Sergei then announced that I could now feel at home.

From the confident manner in which Sergei drove the car I concluded that he was not a newcomer to Berlin—he was apparently living there permanently.

We arrived in Karlshorst, the suburb of Berlin where Soviet military headquarters, Soviet military intelligence, and the offices of the KGB were situated. In a three-room apartment that was, I gathered, kept especially for guests like me, we found a table already laid with the finest Russian food. Zoya, the woman in charge of the apartment, who also worked for the KGB, had really outdone herself: the smell of thick, fatty vegetable soup tickled the nostrils; the vodka was chilled to the point where the bottles were covered with ice; the caviar was visibly fresh; and my favorite Siberian dish—*pelmeni*—had been prepared. The food was steaming hot. The aspic was decorated with green leaves. And, there were sardines, salted cucumbers, crab meat, marinated mushrooms and cheesecakes. It had been a long time since I had seen such a rich display.

Four of us sat down to eat—Sergei, Zoya and a young man by the name of Zhenya who performed the duties of a bodyguard, and me.

Not a word about our business was spoken throughout the evening, of course, although Zoya and Zhenya obviously realized that I was someone from "over there."

As we parted Sergei warned me, "Tomorrow I'll come at nine o'clock and we'll start work. To start with, you will recall for us everything that has happened to you during the past four years. Everything—day by day. Bear in mind that the most insignificant details are important for us. We shall be talking for two or three days—for as long as necessary. Meanwhile, have a rest."

With that he departed. That evening I experienced an unusual feeling of complete relaxation. So that was what it meant, apparently, to be at peace. It was the long forgotten atmosphere of the family home, the absence of danger, the safety of childhood. When I looked more closely I discovered that the apartment had all the features of a typical Soviet home: rusty pipes in the toilet and bathrooms, ugly wallpaper, old-fashioned furniture, loose flooring in the kitchen, and creaky parquet in the rooms. It didn't upset me, rather it contributed to my mental relaxation. I looked around the apartment and recalled Moscow, my parents, and my youth, which had been cut short so unexpectedly.

Fate

I was born "with my shirt on," which according to popular belief means a happy life. From childhood all my relatives assured me of this, but it was a long time before I could make out where the shirt was and what it looked like. When at last, as a young man, I discovered that the shirt was simply the placenta protecting the infant, I experienced a sort of disappointment.

It would be wrong of me to complain about my career. To be born and spend my childhood years practically in the center of Moscow, next to the Belorussia railroad station and to escape many of the postwar problems that accompanied the lives of the majority of my generation—that was no small success.

The house in which I was born is still there, at the beginning of Leningrad Avenue, but none of the original occupants are there now. Our apartment, like most of the others, was a "communal" one. We, the Tumanovs (my parents, my elder bother Igor, my grandmother Pelagea, and I) occupied two rooms. Two other smaller rooms belonged to the Simonovs. And the five poverty-stricken Volkovs occupied only one room. The head of that family, an invalid known as "old Stepa," was a great gambler who was always losing money on the horses. He was let into the house only on those rare occasions when he had been lucky at the races and had not managed to spend all his winnings on drink on the way home. Because of the lack of space, Stepa's mother, grandma Matrena, slept in our common kitchen, where she had her personal storage chest. She went to bed after the last housewife had left the kitchen and rose before anyone when it was still dark.

Grandma Matrena earned her living by rising very early and taking a place in a queue for a shop selling scarce goods and then selling her place to someone else. She could not, of course, buy the goods herself because, apart from the chest in the kitchen, she had no possessions.

Incredible as it may seem, their poverty did not drive any of our neighbors in the apartment into depression. Yes, some of us slept on folding beds and had poor diets, but we also had a "luxury"—a loudspeaker hanging in the corridor played stirring military marches and songs from early morning on. We Tumanovs lived slightly better than the others. For example, we did not cook with foul-smelling cheap fat, but with butter or margarine, which others could not always afford.

Neither we nor our neighbors spent much time reflecting on our poverty for the simple reason that nobody knew anything different. There was nothing to compare our life with. The Soviet way of life was considered to be the best, the richest, and the fairest. Day and night the radio assured us of this, newspapers wrote about it, and teachers told their pupils about it. Anyone who had doubts was quickly "purged" by the authorities and the "vermin" had his ideas corrected. Incidentally, by the time I was born, all of the doubters had probably been rooted out, because in the course of my childhood I never met such "free-thinkers."

On the contrary, according the radio, people living in the West were exploited by a gang of capitalist vampires and eked out a miserable existence, starving, oppressed, and deprived of their rights. We were genuinely sorry for the "ordinary people" of the Capitalist countries, especially the negroes who, to judge by the propaganda, were the most unfortunate and oppressed. We regarded the negroes as "class brothers."

Knowledge does not always bring happiness. Perhaps it was good that we did not know in what poverty we lived.

During the war my father served in the NKVD—the forerunner of the KGB. I never knew what position he occupied or what he did, for he never said anything about his war service. I can only guess that he was involved in counterintelligence. In 1948, for some unknown reason, he left the Lubyanka (the secret police headquarters) and went to work in a variety of enterprises as a specialist in personnel questions.

My mother was also employed in the state security organization at the rank of senior lieutenant, although she actually worked in one of the military commissariats. My brother, who was twelve years older than I, became a member of the Moscow University's geology faculty after finishing school. He worked in that field to his obvious satisfaction until he retired.

I would not have distinguished myself in any way from the other students at the boys' school No. 155—situated next to the "Wings of the Soviets" sports club—if it had not been for an escapade that drew immediate attention to a nine-year-old lad and made him famous for a time. What happened was this. I persuaded two of my friends to escape with me to Africa, and in February 1954, we threw away our school books, left our parents a note ("Do not look for us—we have gone forever."), caught a train, and set off from Moscow in a southerly direction. My neighbor in the apartment, Sashka Simonov, for some reason took with him to Africa a pair of warm winter felt boots, which he clutched to himself the whole way. Our journey did not last long: the next morning, somewhere beyond Kaluga, the police caught us and returned us to our very worried parents.

Sashka, whose mother worked as a warden in the Butyrki prison, was beaten so mercilessly and screamed so loudly that people living on all floors in the building shook with fright. My parents, however, were so pleased that their "prodigal son" had returned that I was welcomed with cakes—so many as I have never seen since.

My welcome at school was not, however, quite so warm: the school-mistress decided at once that I was the initiator of the "crime," threatened to "throw me out," and thereafter treated me with great suspicion. "We don't need such pupils," she said in a threatening tone, giving me an icy look.

I reached bottom in the schoolmistress' eyes when some boys beat up the son of the *Pravda* columnist, Victor Mayevsky. Mayevsky was a journalist who belonged to the top party *nomenklatura* and had access to the very narrow circle of people who were permitted to make regular trips abroad. Like all people close to the center of power, he and his family were not short of money. Mayevsky's son Zhenka would bring ham sandwiches and smoked sausage to school for lunch and would then eat them demonstratively—to the envy of all the other boys, most of whom could at best afford only a pastry with cabbage.

On one occasion, one of the particularly poor children, who apparently could simply no longer stand to look at Zhenka's well-fed, self-satisfied face, struck the "bourgeois" Zhenka. For some reason the headmaster of the school decided that the incident could not have happened without my being involved. My unsuccessful attempt to get to Africa had fixed me in his mind as a criminal type.

"Do you know who the father of this boy is?" he inquired menacingly of our class, but looking for some reason at me. "Do you know that comrade Stalin himself shakes his hand? And you dare to make fun of this boy. We'll send you off to prison, to labor colonies. To Siberia! To Kolyma! Beyond the Arctic Circle!"

No. The headmaster was definitely never going to forgive me for the lighthearted trip to Africa. He was probably one of those people for whom anyone who stepped out of the general faceless mass automatically came under suspicion. The Stalinist regime depended on people like him. Fortunately, the next year I moved to a different school from which I graduated satisfactorily in 1961.

It was there that I met my bosom friend Tolik Yesiava. His father, after surviving the labor camps and exile, had been given permission to live in Moscow. To be precise, Tolik's father was not a victim of Stalin's terror in the true sense of the word. Ever since prewar days the elder Yesiava had occupied a very high position on the staff of the "leader of the peoples"—he had been in charge of the transport department of the government bodyguard. Yesiava had at his disposal everything Stalin might need for a trip—motor cars, trains, speed boats, and aircraft. One can imagine just how powerful the man was as a high-ranking officer in the state security and what a comfortable childhood was awaiting Tolik.

Everything collapsed, however, in a single day. One day Tolik's father, in the company of other secret policemen, had a drunken party in a restaurant on the Akhun mountain near Sochi. After the party, Tolik's father—a man normally capable of driving any form of transport except a plane—sat behind the wheel of an open-topped Packard to drive the whole company down the zigzagging mountain road. The car shot off the road and down the mountain. Some in the party were killed, some were injured. Stalin's favorite, Yesiava, however, was alive and unharmed. He was sent to prison.

They say that when Stalin heard about the incident, he spoke only one sentence: "If Yesiava is to blame, he must be punished." That very night Tolik's entire family was moved from their luxurious apartment in the center of Moscow and all of their valuables were confiscated. When I met and became friends with Tolik, he was living with his father in a communal apartment just like ours. Tolik's father died in 1956.

Of all the hobbies of my childhood, the one that stuck with me the longest was photography. I would never be parted from my camera at home or at school. By the time I was fifteen, I had gained the reputation of being the school's official photographer. When the headmaster transformed a restroom on the school's third floor into a photographic laboratory my status improved further. Although I was only a pupil, I became the possessor of the key to my own room. Photography and producing school wall newspapers not only provided me with personal satisfaction, but also gave me special privileges—the value of which I soon came to realize. With the excuse of having urgent work in the laboratory I could easily skip any of the less important subjects, such as physical culture, drawing, and military studies. And, when everyone else was running cross-country races, I was permitted to stand importantly at the finish line snapping pictures of the runners.

During the summer holidays I was sent to the country to stay with grandma Domna, my father's mother. Before the war the village where she lived had consisted of about fifty cottages. After the war, only six remained: the rest were burned down by the Germans as they retreated. Despite this shocking fact, grandma Domna, to my amazement, always spoke with respect of the occupying Germans alongside whom she had lived for more than two years. The Germans had turned my grandmother's house into a field hospital. She was required to carry water from the well and boil it on her stove—jobs for which the surgeon paid her in foodstuffs. "If it had not been for the kind German," she recalled, "we would have turned up our toes from hunger."

In 1943, when the great advance of Soviet troops along the whole front began, the Germans tried to hold this region in a pincer movement. Fierce battles flared up. Soviet planes carried out a bombing raid on the village in which, apart from the hospital, was situated the military headquarters. My grandfather was wounded in the leg by a piece of shrapnel, and it was again the "kind German" who operated on him. Thus, my relatives had no complaints about the German army. They did, however, curse the Gestapo and special troops with the worst words they knew, for it was they who had burnt everything in sight as they retreated. Our cottage survived only because, right up to the last minute, the wounded were being operated on and the SS just did not have time to set it alight.

A year and a half before we finished the ten-year school, Tolik Yesiava found me something else to do. At the time, Tolik was working in an operational Komsomol unit that had been set up for a campaign to deal with young criminals and hooligans. He persuaded me to join the same unit, adding that they had great need of a good photographer.

It was fate. That day marked the beginning of my career as a spy working abroad.

Ivan Ivanovich in Charge

If I am not mistaken, the origin of the operational Komsomol units was connected with the World Festival of Youth and Students, which took place in Moscow is 1957. Until then the majority of Moscovites had seen foreigners only in newspapers or at the cinema. For many years the "Country of Soviets" had lived behind an absolutely impenetrable "iron curtain," and anyone who was so careless as to receive a letter with a foreign date stamp was sent to prison or even executed "for espionage."

The idea of inviting the festival to be held in the Soviet Union appealed very much to Nikita Khrushchev, then leader of the Soviet Union, who had the year before, at the Twentieth Congress of the Communist Party, branded Stalin's regime criminal, and was interested in improving the reputation of Bolshevism in the eyes of the world. I can only imagine the horror of officials who were ordered to involve themselves directly with the organization of the festival, and above all that of the employees of the state security organization. Previously every single (!) foreign citizen had been kept under close observation, but now Moscow was expecting several thousand guests, from around the world, at once. How could you know which of them was working for the special services? How could they all be kept under observation? How could they be prevented from making undesirable contacts with Moscovites?

Even if the security forces in the capital were to be supported by people from outside Moscow, it would still be impossible to keep track of every participant in the festival. Moreover, Khrushchev issued instructions that the police were to work more circumspectly, not to offend the visitors, but rather to demonstrate the "real Russian hospitality."

In short, the stern characters in their offices on Dzerzhinsky Square had to do some serious thinking. One of them had an idea: what about calling in the more politically aware section of Soviet youth as assistants, that is, actual participants of the forthcoming festival—Moscow students, schoolchildren, and young workers? Select the most reliable, explain their task to them, form them into groups, and attach the leaders of the groups to "advisors" from the KGB. Let the young people have a good time at the festival and at the same time keep a watchful eye both on their own people and the foreigners. If they saw anything suspicious they were to report to the KGB.

The idea pleased the leaders so much that after the World Festival had been successfully concluded, orders were given for the same regime to be introduced everywhere—from Moscow to the very outskirts of the

Soviet Union. The young people's enthusiasm was skillfully exploited to purge the country of its criminal elements. The operational units were ordered to organize a campaign against hooliganism, currency dealers, and prostitution. They were used to keep crowds back during police raids and to keep order during major political occasions, like the demonstrations in Red Square.

In the big cities, especially if they were visited by foreigners, the work of such units was directed by the KGB; in others it was handled by the police or the criminal investigation department. Moreover, they were all used as a reliable reserve of manpower: officers of the KGB and police had time to study their young assistants and to recommend the best of them for training in the appropriate institutions of the KGB and the MVD. The majority of today's generals and colonels got their start as young men with romantic ideas they formed in the operational units that battled with the hooligans during the late 1950s and early 1960s.

Some former "operatives" may have done things in their past for which they are ashamed—there's a black sheep in every family—but I have nothing in my distant past to make me blush. I, and other members of the Komsomol units, thank goodness, did not spy on foreigners, nor keep an eye on Soviet dissidents. Rather, our main task was to keep order in the center of Moscow, and to "cleanse" the cafés, restaurants, and hotels of hooligans. Our job was to prevent foreign guests of the capital from being bothered by the persistent pestering of prostitutes, and to put a stop to currency dealing and the sale and use of drugs. One of the reasons that we kept an eye on the prostitutes was to ensure that the "right prostitutes," got into the hotels—the ladies who worked for the KGB. We chased away the others.

The various kinds of long-term supervision, arrests, and interrogations did not come within our competence—they were the business of the police or KGB. We were sort of auxiliaries, a kind of "light cavalry."

As a young man nearing the end of my school days, I enjoyed being involved in the totally adult and semi-secret business of the Komsomol. I felt myself a more important figure than the rest of my friends who were not allowed to enter the "secret order" of the operatives. We were issued identity cards and permits that said "entry everywhere," and once, after an especially successful raid on currency dealers, were rewarded with articles that had been confiscated. I received a shirt and tie—my only reward for three years' work.

Now, of course, I can be reproached with questions such as: "What have you got to boast about? Were you not fighting people of your own generation?" To this I reply: Yes, I fought them, but they were the people I would still consider to be scum and vermin. Incidentally, we were also given the task of "re-educating" our clients and drawing those who had gone astray into the process of "actively building communism." As I recall, our unit was responsible for supervising the behaviors of two young girls of loose morals—Stella and Ella. These healthy, fun-loving, silly twins worked in a factory. When they were done working, they were required to report to our headquarters at the end of Gorky Street, opposite what is now the Intourist Hotel, and help with keeping the records of the operational unit. In my opinion, the more energetic young operatives did with the twins—when they were not occupied with this boring work—what other girls were paid to do in the hotels.

Stella and Ella did not complain. The process of "re-education" suited them much better than being forced to live 100 kilometers from Moscow, which was, at the time, the most frequent punishment for prostitutes, alcoholics, and petty hooligans.

It sometimes happened that the "re-education" process took on a more refined character. I remember that one summer, after catching a couple of hooligans, we stuffed their pants full of nettles and put them on a train with the parting words, "Don't get caught again."

Perhaps these actions do not accord very well with the principles of democracy and the declaration on the rights of man, but anyone would confirm that there was far more order in Moscow in those days than there is today. During those years we really put the hooligans' noses out of joint and you could safely wander around the capital at any time of day or night. Now, it is wiser not to leave home without a gun after eight o'clock at night. The "model Communist city," as Moscow was called until recently, has become a dirty collection of profiteers, drug addicts, prostitutes, and racketeers.

I stopped working with the operational unit at the end of May 1961, when it was time to sit for my final examinations at school. It was then that I really got down to my studies and even reckoned on getting a silver medal for my examination results—which would have made it much easier for me to be admitted to college later. My future had already been decided. I would go to the Institute of Cinematography and enter the faculty for cameramen.

In the middle of the examinations, however, I received a phone call from the headquarters of the operational unit. "Come over here, Ivan Ivanovich wants to meet you."

There was no need to explain who Ivan Ivanovich Zaitsev was. He never told anyone what his job was, but everyone in the unit knew that he was in the KGB and was in charge of us. Thus, we didn't ask too many questions.

Ivan Ivanovich Zaitsev was always surrounded with an air of mystery. He did not condescend to meet and talk with every member of the unit. He was the personification of the institution that one did not refer to aloud. We usually avoided mention of his function, instead talking vaguely of the "office," the "committee," or silently patting our shoulders—where epaulets are worn.

Now this man was inviting me "for a chat." Why, suddenly? Perhaps he wished to find out why I had stopped working for the unit. Lost in conjecture, I arrived at headquarters for a conversation that was to take place with no one else present, and which would probably have appeared rather strange to an observer.

Ivan Ivanovich politely invited me to take a seat. He checked to see that the door was properly closed and remained standing. Then he picked up the papers from the desk and put them into an old-fashioned leather briefcase with metal clasps. The plate on the case was inscribed with the words, "To I. I. Zaitsev, for work with young people." It was said that he had been presented with the briefcase as a reward by Shelepin, the head of the KGB. As I looked at Zaitsev, I thought, this elderly, rather wilted man looks more like a provincial bookkeeper than an active secret policeman.

"So how are the exams going?"—he began the conversation from afar. "Were you well prepared for them?"

"Not too bad it seems."

"You really are a good lad. You find time for everything. Incidentally, Oleg, what are you thinking of doing when you finish school? What plans have you?"

I told him about my desire to learn to be a film cameraman.

"Good idea!" He again gave the impression that he was genuinely pleased with me. "But bear in mind that the competition to enter the cinematography institute is tremendous. If you finish school with a medal it's all right, but if not . . . by the way, why must it be cinematography?"

I reminded him that I had long made photography my hobby and that I had already made an amateur film.

"Yes, yes, photography is very good," Ivan Ivanovich agreed. "But have you not thought about any other profession?"

"What kind of profession?"

"Well . . . " he waved his arms about vaguely. "Let us say something connected with working abroad."

"No," I confessed honestly. "I have not thought of that."

"There you are," for some reason it seemed to cheer him. "You have not thought of it. But you should. Don't be in too much of a hurry, my friend.

Think it over and weigh things out. Then make up your mind."

But I had already made my decision, and as soon as the exams were over (unfortunately, I was far from getting a medal) I set off to deliver my application to the Institute of Cinematography. I attached to the application what appeared to me to be my especially successful photographs, as well as a short amateur film that I had shot with an 8-millimeter Admira camera. I thought that would be enough to persuade the selection committee that I obviously had talent. For some reason, I had practically no doubt that I would do well in the competition and pass the examination.

Alas . . . it was in that very year that the tireless reformer, Nikita Khrushchev, issued an instruction that before students could be accepted at most of the country's institutes they would have to have two years of employment or service in the army behind them. Our leader believed, naïvely, that young people who, before their education, had worked in a collective farm or factory, or had experienced the smell of soldiers' socks, would make better use of a course in science. Apart from that—and this could only be welcomed—he wanted it that way to defeat the awful Soviet disease known as *blat,* which meant that children of highly placed officials benefitted from the protection of their important parents and had no difficulty getting into the most prestigious institutes, thus blocking the road for others. Khrushchev was now sending everyone to work in factories, including me.

My documents were returned to me from the selection commission of the institute with the request that I reapply in not less than two years and that with my application I include proof that I had been employed. They also advised me to work at something related to my future profession.

I immediately went to the studios of Mosfilm, where I was instantly hired as an assistant cameraman. My duties were fairly simple—carry the camera and other equipment in the wake of the cameraman, and do some other minor jobs. I was paid at the rate of sixty rubles a month for this undemanding work. I had more or less come to terms with the job when my parents suddenly intervened.

"No regular working day?" my mother asked with suspicion in her voice. "That means you will be coming home when you feel like it? When you're only 16? Oh no, I don't like that sort of job."

"The cinema," my father supported her gloomily. "Parties. Drinking. Women. Debauchery."

My choice of job probably did really upset my father to the depths of his being. But sometimes I wonder if he was not in some way set on a different future that had been prepared for me in which there was no place for filmmaking. Perhaps, as an officer in the secret police, he had been entrusted with part of the secret plans for me, or they had conferred with him about me, or they had simply hinted . . . I don't know. In any case, a few weeks later I was dismissed from Mosfilm. They had received a letter from my parents and immediately took leave of me forever. With that, I said goodbye to my dream of being a cinematographer.

At the headquarters of the operational unit they passed me a request from Ivan Ivanovich to call at the Hotel Sovietskaya and go to a room rented by the KGB on the second floor. Most of the hotels in Moscow had similar special rooms, which were intended for meetings between KGB officers and their agents, for recruiting new helpers, and for other secret business.

The room appeared to be a normal hotel room — though it was not unlikely that it was equipped with special recording apparatus. I was again welcomed by our "keeper."

"Sit down, Oleg. Let's have a talk. Smoke if you wish."

Ivan Ivanovich was dressed modestly in clothes of Soviet manufacture. As I was to learn later, he did not smoke and avoided strong drink.

"So, my friend, they couldn't make a cameraman out of you?" He immediately demonstrated how well informed he was. "Only you mustn't get upset for no reason. Work in films is nonsense. No work for a real man. We," and he put great emphasis on the "we," "have been studying you for a long time. You're good at 'sambo,' a good shot, and an outstanding photographer. And you have a good reputation in the unit. No, Oleg, you have a different future ahead of you than films."

When I heard these words I honestly thought: surely they don't want me to got to a spy school. But at that point, for the first time, he took me by surprise.

"You, my friend, are going to the C.A. Institute."

"The what?" I jumped up in surprise.

"The Institute of Civil Aviation," he stressed each word separately to make it clear.

"Don't be in a hurry to turn it down," Ivan Ivanovich was laughing good-heartedly at me. "You won't get into the film institute anyway, do you realize that?"

I nodded, having grasped that for me to go to the film institute did not for some reason fit *their* plans, and that naturally meant that I should forget it once and for all.

"That's right," he agreed with satisfaction. "But why in that case should you hang around doing nothing, pretending to work somewhere? No my friend, that wouldn't do. The aviation institute takes people who have not been employed anywhere. They have only to go through a medical commission and take an examination. You will be studying the speciality 'aviation radio equipment.' And when you've completed your studies, we," again putting significant emphasis on the *we*, "promise interesting prospects."

I would like to see a single seventeen-year-old lad who in those days would dare to argue with a man from the secret police. If they wanted something, that's how it had to be. They knew best.

"All right then," I said. "Where do I hand in my documents?"

He dictated the address of the selection commission and said that the medical examination took place in a special military building next to the Dynamo stadium.

"It's where all the airmen are checked," he explained.

To my great surprise the most difficult part of what I then had to go through was the medical check-up. For five days I was chased from one doctor to another. They prodded me and X-rayed me, tortured me on machines, shut me into chambers, and spun me around in a centrifuge. It was as though I was going to be an astronaut and not to work in civil aviation. Finally I was handed the required decision: "Fit for flying duties without limitation."

Although the institute I was to enter was in Kiev, the visiting examination commission worked at the central aerodrome in Moscow. (I only had to travel about five stops on the trolley-bus to get from where I lived to take the entrance examinations.) I received quite good marks on the mathematics examination, and my aggregate result was quite satisfactory. So I was already congratulating myself on my learning before the list of successful candidates was posted. When I read the list, however, my name did not appear. I spent a long time looking through the lists, believing at first that there was some misunderstanding or that my name had been left out through carelessness. Others who had received worse marks than mine were on the list. But I was not.

I strolled home along Leningrad Avenue trying to figure out what it meant. To tell the truth, I didn't feel very sorry—I had never been drawn to the sky and I had never understood technology, so my failure did not lie on my heart like a heavy stone. But the disappointment and the bewilderment at what had happened remained.

For some time I had occasionally begun to feel that I was a toy in someone's powerful hands. I was going to have to get used to it.

After having hurled my mathematics textbook into a corner, I told my family, "All the same, I'll get into the film institute. They will never make a pilot of me."

"Now, now," my father muttered uncertainly.

The next day Ivan Ivanovich reappeared. Hanging my head, I tried to explain to him: it was a disaster, nothing had come out of his plan, please forgive me. But he did not even pretend to be disappointed.

"Don't hang your head, my young friend. There is no reason to grieve. Of course, aviation is very attractive, but you haven't lost everything yet."

I looked at him as you look at a juggler in the circus. What was the next trick he had up his sleeve? He hadn't summoned me to console me.

"Oleg, you go and do some work, that's what I have to tell you. Not just anywhere, but at a 'postbox.' It is, as it happens, not far from where you live and it is also connected to aviation. Work there for a while, recover your strength, and then we'll see."

Ivan Ivanovich had the ability to give the impression that he didn't notice how he confused the person he was talking to. Every time we met he pulled the rug from under me without batting an eyelid. He explained to me in a businesslike fashion where the "postbox" was, to whom I was to report, and even the job I was going to do. It appeared that I was to be a draftsman.

Really! I had gotten into Mosfilm. I had the possibility of a pleasant profession as a cameraman and of entering a much sought-after institute. Now they wanted me to be shut up in some lousy postbox, sit behind a drawing board, and work for fixed hours every day. No, not that!

I looked him in the face. "You know, if it's all the same, I would like to devote my life to making films."

"Really?" He looked surprised, as though it was the first time he had heard about it. Then unexpectedly he switched to an official voice: "Well, Oleg Alexandrovich, in our country everyone is free to choose for himself a profession according to his own wishes. And you are, of course, no exception, but I would recommend that you soberly assess your real possibilities. Soberly! Do you understand?"

And so that it should be more understandable to me, he concluded with the uttermost frankness, "You will never, never, get into the film institute. Is that clear?"

And again we sat chatting like a couple of old friends—one young and the other elderly. The young one obediently took in the words of the older man. Ivan Ivanovich advised me not to give up my physical training and to continue to take part in the work of the operational unit. Finally, he said that we should probably meet again soon.

"You don't have any objections to our meeting, do you?" He patted me on the shoulder as we parted. "Only there's one thing not to forget—no other living being in the world must know about these meetings."

It remained forever a mystery to me why *they* made all the fuss about my entering the institute of civil aviation. I can think of only one reasonable explanation. Before entering into some major affair, they wanted to carefully check out my state of health. So they chose a very winding road to do it. I have no doubt that *they* received a detailed and lengthy report on all aspects of my health, including my psychological stability, from the secret medical department in the Dynamo stadium. Well, if that was it, one had to give someone's inventiveness its due.

It was then that my grandfather, who had not visited for a long time, reappeared in our home. He had served in the Ninth Directorate of the KGB with the rank of colonel and had retired as a general. The Ninth Directorate was concerned with the protection of top party and state officials. Because of their proximity to top people, officers in that directorate always appeared to be in a special position and looked down on everybody else. That continued, incidentally, right up until August 1991. After the attempt to overthrow Gorbachev, the Ninth Directorate was given a good shaking up and was removed from the organization of state security.

Strange as it may seem, my grandfather also supported the idea of my working at "postbox" No. 1303 and had surprisingly detailed knowledge about the place where I was to work. It turned out to be the aircraft design bureau named after Yakovlev, and an experimental workshop where designers' ideas were transformed into real aircraft. I was to work in what was known as the "wing brigade."

In August 1961, I delivered an application to the personnel department with a request to be transferred to the design bureau and a detailed questionnaire that listed all of my relatives almost back to my great grandmothers.

"You have come from Sergei Illyich?" the elderly woman in the personnel department asked me politely.

"Yes," I replied, as I had been taught, not having the slightest idea who this Sergei Illyich was. Three days later I was issued a pass and told what my work would consist of. The pay was just fifty rubles a month—ten less than at Mosfilm.

At the time the Yakovlev bureau was having some difficulties. For many years the aircraft industry had not received anything new from it. The aircraft designer Yakovlev, famous in the past and a favorite of Stalin's, had created a series of outstanding fighter aircraft during the 1930s and 1940s, but this collective of many thousands of people was in serious crisis. Even I, a mere lad and an apprentice draftsman, could feel it. People worked in a slipshod manner, and everything bore the imprint of decline, dull routine, and drabness.

I cannot say that I was seriously upset on this account. The design bureau was an intermediate station on my path and I had the feeling that the future held many disturbing surprises for me. No one overloaded me with work and I could leave long before the end of the working day on the excuse that I had to report to the operational unit. Nobody gave a damn where I was or what I was doing.

Ivan Ivanovich reappeared only six months later. We met in the same impersonal room on the second floor of the Hotel Sovietskaya.

"Do you remember our previous talks, Oleg?"—he asked, surveying me attentively from head to toe.

"Of course, only it's already time for me to be thinking about my military service. I will be called up soon."

"That's true," said my mentor approvingly. "The time has come for you to carry out your sacred duty in the defense of your motherland. And in the meantime," he spoke without pausing as though he did not care what effects his words would have, "In the meantime, you will go and take preparatory courses at a certain institute."

What sort of surprise had my old friend prepared for me now? I tried to contain my curiosity, but the question burst out involuntarily.

"What institute this time?"

"The most prestigious," the secret policeman said calmly. "The MGIMO [MGIMO stands for the Moscow State Institute for International Relations, which trains diplomats and specialists in international economics]. Have you heard of it?"

"I've heard of it all right, but I never thought I would study there."

"Well you will, you will," he promised. "What is more, you will go abroad to work. But first you must complete the preparatory courses that exist especially for young people from the workplace. There you will improve your English and work on other things. You have probably forgotten everything since you left school?"

"I am forgetting," I agreed. "But this is all rather unexpected. Courses at the MGIMO and . . . "

"You'll get used to it, my friend. We have a lot of surprises ahead."

What can I say about such a meeting? I suppose it's this: In an indirect way Ivan Ivanovich had let me understand that he was well informed about my affairs. I believe he even knew the name of the girl I was then going out with. Even in his words of praise I could detect the amazing extent to which he was informed. "Good lad," he said, "they are satisfied with you at work and you've got reliable friends."

Along with several other boys and girls from the KGB, I was soon accepted for courses in the institute without any difficulty. I then began to prepare myself for joining the faculty of international economics.

Dreams of the film institute had finally been laid to rest. The institute of civil aviation also seemed just a strange dream. Now I was conscientiously paving the way toward a career working abroad.

The courses were held in the evenings in the institute's main building near the Crimea bridge (where the diplomatic academy is now). I studied English, geography, mathematics, and the fundamentals of economics. Gradually I caught up with the others. To tell the truth, however, I had difficulty imagining what my future held. Perhaps subconsciously I realized that my future now depended very little on myself. I felt as though I was swimming vigorously with the current, not knowing where the waves would carry me. But I had no fear of going to the bottom.

Ivan Ivanovich reminded me of his existence in mid-summer 1963. This time the meeting took place in a café opposite the watch factory next to Belorussia station. Apparently my mentor's bosses in the KGB were taking me seriously for they had permitted Zaitsev to spend government money on a meal for three. The third person at our table turned out to be Ivanovich's young colleague, a smartly dressed young man by the name of Sergei. Introducing us, Ivan Ivanovich warned me that in the future, Sergei would possibly be having regular meetings with me. On this occasion, however, Sergei studied me very closely but remained mostly silent.

The older man ordered brandies for us and a Georgian wine for himself. (In those days in Moscow good dry wines were being sold everywhere and cost only kopeks.) We drank and exchanged some pleasantries. It had been a long time since our last meeting, but I felt that there was no point in telling them about my life because they already knew all about it. In any case, my mentor did not ask me about anything. With our previous meetings in mind, I was determined not to be surprised at anything and determined to appear imperturbable, as was proper for an experienced spy. But Ivan Ivanovich once again knocked me off my perch.

"Listen," he said. "Oleg, what have you gained by being at the institute of international relations? Don't you think, my friend, that it is time for you to leave it?"

"What's that?" In a flash all of my assumed coolness left me. "What on earth are you talking about? I've got my entrance exams any day now. I've been preparing for them for eighteen months. I've even caught up in mathematics."

But my protest did not make the slightest impression on them. "Forget it," said Zaitsev with a dismissive wave of his hand, as though it was a matter of no importance. "Better drink up your brandy and listen to me.

Supposing you do graduate from that institute, what then? Do you think that they are going to send you abroad immediately to Paris, London, New York? No my friend, it wouldn't work like that. Very few actually go abroad—those who are lucky or have some protection—the rest get jobs as teachers. Do you want to be a teacher?"

I shook my head.

"You don't, and you are quite right. We have other plans for you . . . "

"But after all it was you who advised me to get into the institute."

"Forget it," he repeated, now rather more sharply, passing over my reproach without comment. "You are going into the army. Actually, into the navy. You are a good fighter. You will do your military service and develop your strength, and then we shall see. There's interesting work ahead for you—you won't regret it. But you had ideas about being a diplomat or an economic adviser . . . No way!"

I didn't remind him that it was he, not I, who had had those ideas. But I couldn't refrain from asking, "What sort of work will there be?"

It sounded a childish question and was evidence that I had given in once again. He smiled and tipped some more brandy into my glass.

"All in good time. You will be told later. Meanwhile, expect to receive your call-up papers and prepare for your military service."

I made one more pathetic attempt to get myself out of the situation, muttering something about the good chance I had of being admitted to the institute and the teachers' high opinions of me. But all that was apparently of no importance. It was as if a powerful gust of wind had picked me up from the track I was on and carried me off to goodness knows where.

I recall now, that when I collected my documents from the institute's selection commission, they eyed me as though out of my mind. They already regarded me practically as a student—the examinations were a mere formality for those of us who were taking the preparatory courses.

"You do realize what you are doing?" the woman who handed me my documents asked in amazement. "You'll never get a second chance."

I muttered something meaningless in reply. And with that the doors of the most prestigious institute were slammed behind me.

First they had told me to forget about the film business. Then they had gotten me involved with aircraft. And now they had grabbed me by the scruff of the neck and dragged me away from the entrance to the institute from which there was a direct road into diplomatic service. What was the point of it all? What sort of secret work was the KGB preparing me for? And why did it have to be approached through such a strange and winding road?

A Baltic Sailor

At the beginning of September I received a summons requiring "Citizen Tumanov, Oleg Alexandrovich, in accordance with the law of the USSR 'concerning obligatory military service' to report for service." It indicated that I was to enter into command No. 141. My mother attempted, by making use of her former connections with the military, to find out what sort of a command this was and where I was likely to be sent, but they would not tell her.

On the fifth of September, I took leave of my friends and relations, and along with the other young men entering the military, got into a bus at Begovaya Street—the assembly point for Krasnaya Presnya and . . . the transit prison. I don't know what they do now, but in those days it was there that they assembled the recruits.

Our heads were shaved and our clothes were put into special chambers to be steamed. Then we were loaded into a train guarded by armed sailors. Soon the word was passed down—we were going to the Kaliningrad region, the former East Prussia, to join the Baltic fleet.

In Pioneerska, next to the naval airbase, we were distributed among the various commands. Some were sent to serve in the border troops, others were put into naval uniform. I was informed that I would be serving in the shipborne artillery.

Where I served was all the same to me. Civilian life was now left behind somewhere in the distant past and four painful years of military service lay ahead. There was nothing for me to do but get used to my new state. I was firmly determined not to take anything to heart, but to treat everything with Olympian composure—no matter what happened. If they ordered me to be an artillery man—fine! If they wanted me to serve in submarines—excellent! If the engine department wanted me to join the greasy mechanics—that's what I had dreamt of all my life!

After a few days our team of future minelayers and gunners was packed into a train and transported even closer to the Polish border to the little town of Mamonov, formerly the German Heiledenbeil. The place was surrounded by a forbidden zone and all along the roads were gateways behind which were military units, parade grounds, teaching bases, and rocket emplacements. It was possibly the most heavily militarized place in the whole of the USSR.

In the study center they started to prepare me for service with the group that calculated the aiming of artillery fire, which aboard ship was considered to be an elite body. It meant handling complicated calculations, using primitive electronics, which were then only in the early stages of use in the USSR.

We lived in old German barracks, left from the time when Hitler's famous "Viking" tank division had been quartered there. I will remember all my life the long corridors that I frequently had to swab at night—the usual punishment for disciplinary infractions in the Soviet Army and Fleet. Incidentally, the other form of punishment was no better: offenders were sent to the galley and made to peel potatoes for everybody.

"That's so that your service shouldn't seem to be too easy," the bad-tempered sergeant would say each time he punished me for some innocent act.

It seemed that the sergeant was not very fond of recruits from Moscow. He found them too literate. There were only three Moscovites in the company of "artillery aimers."

As the spring approached we began to guess where we would be sent to serve after completing our training. Men were sent from there to the Baltic, the Black Sea, and even the Arctic fleet. According to talk among the sailors the most frightful place to serve was aboard the cruiser *Sverdlov*, which was said to be a floating prison that only thick-skinned Siberians could tolerate, and not all of them survived. Actually, it was mainly men from Siberia who were called to serve on that cruiser, and every two years Siberia sent the crew of the *Sverdlov* a real Siberian bear. With the arrival of the new bear, the previous bear, by then full grown, would be put ashore or given to a zoo.

Now the study course was behind me. All of us newly trained gunners and minelayers were drawn up on the parade ground and each was told where he was being sent for the continuation of his service.

"Seaman Tumanov—to the one hundred and sixty-fifth brigade of rocket ships."

For goodness sake! That was to the place where the leading ship was the cruiser *Sverdlov*. Was I really going to serve on that floating prison? No, I was in luck; from the brigade headquarters in Baltisk I was sent to the destroyer *Spravedlivy*.

After looking around the vessel I quickly realized that I could greatly benefit by making use of some civilian skills, including my skill at photography. I made friends with Valera Shulgin. He had been carrying out the duties of ship's photographer and had only one more year to serve. He took me to the deputy captain to tell him: "Look, comrade captain, I've found a replacement. I am soon to go ashore, let this chap get used to the job."

From that point on my military service became a great deal easier. While others were being bored at political lectures, I was developing film in the photographic laboratory, or designing the wall newspaper. Moreover, all of them, including the long-service men, treated me with respect because they all wanted to send photos of themselves home—see what a fine sailor I am!

On top of that, the navigation officer got to know about my work as an apprentice draftsman and was delighted.

"Sailor Tumanov," he said, "you are a real find for me. You will now be drawing the maps and other navigational drawings."

He was a lazy fellow and rejoiced at any possibility of shifting his work to someone else. And what difference did it make to me? I was getting through my military service. I would tell my officer that I had been ordered by the deputy captain of the destroyer quickly to pull together a display about "stars of military and political training" and that, therefore, I not be included in the next watch. I would tell the deputy captain that I had received an urgent task from the navigation officer. And to avoid him, I would shut myself away in the darkroom.

To have a room to oneself on a crowded ship where you keep bumping into each other and to be able to hide oneself away was an unheard of luxury for a seaman in his first year of service. I even had a key to a tiny storeroom that had been equipped as a darkroom.

I did not, of course, abuse that "privilege." Rather, I tried to keep all satisfied with me—the deputy captain, the navigation officer, and my own officer—so that I would not appear to be enjoying special favors.

The officers treated me with even greater respect when brief reports with the signature "Seaman O. Tumanov" began to appear in the navy newspaper *Strazh Baltiki*. Of course, the reports described the various successes of our destroyer. As a freelance correspondent I was able to go ashore practically every day when the ship was at its base—I only had to say that I was on my way to the editorial office.

For such service my officers put me forward for membership in the Communist Party. I didn't object. Membership in the CPSU could always be useful to me in civilian life, and in those days, one could not obtain a decent job without it. So I became a candidate for membership.

In the spring of 1965, the deputy editor of the newspaper advised me to try to get into the higher military-political school in Lvov, where civilian employees were trained for the Armed Forces and as military journalists. The editor of *Strazh Baltiki* painted a vivid picture of the advantages of taking such a step. In the first place, to be taken on for training would mean an end to my service as a sailor, which I had already come to hate. In the second place, he said, the diploma of a military journalist was very highly valued and would save me in any situation. For me, however, what was most attractive was the possibility of getting out of doing my service. From what the editor said, I gathered that if I went for this I would have a month's leave followed by another month to prepare for the examinations for the courses for soldiers and sailors at the school. Perhaps it was worth trying. Two months away from the ship. Almost freedom . . .

And then we would see. To become a military journalist, which meant tying up the rest of my life with the Armed Forces—frankly, I had no intention of doing that.

After the destroyer had taken part in the May Day parade we were informed that it was going to Liepaja for repairs. Many of us, myself included, were sent on leave. I bought a plane ticket and some presents for my parents in Liepaja and was in Moscow by that evening. Three days later there was a phone call.

"Greetings, sailor. Ivan Ivanovich speaking."

"Greetings to you too!" I said, somewhat confused, having forgotten my "keeper" in the two years.

"I know you are doing your service well. Freelance correspondent . . . Candidate for membership in the party . . . Thinking of going to school . . . Very good! But you haven't forgotten our conversations? No? Then let's meet tomorrow and discuss something."

I arrived at the Sovietskaya Hotel at the appointed time. But it was a different room—rather two rooms—well furnished, with carpets and crystal. And Ivan Ivanovich was not alone.

"Get to know each other," Ivan Ivanovich said as the young-looking, smartly dressed man with him rose from his chair to greet me.

"Oleg Maximovich," he introduced himself.

This was my first acquaintance with one of the best "field" operators in KGB's counterintelligence. Later we would meet in secret many times in various cities in Europe, but that comes later in my story.

A man of average height, with the figure of a young man, wearing an expensive, imported suit—this Oleg Maximovich made a powerful impression on me. All of the people from the Lubyanka I had met before looked the same to me—inexpressive and unmemorable. But this man was imposing and relaxed in his behavior. With his dark eyes and thin toothbrush mustache, Oleg Maximovich looked more like a foreigner than a Russian. At his feet was a luxurious attaché case, something practically no one in Moscow had in those days. He chatted with me in a very relaxed manner.

"You do, I hope, realize that I am an employee of the Committee for State Security [KGB]," he warned, after quite openly examining me from head to foot. I nodded.

"Fine. Then for a start, tell us how your military service is going and what plans you have."

I started to tell them, although I was well aware that they already knew everything I would relate. It was just that Oleg Maximovich apparently wanted to form a more complete impression of me.

"But perhaps you would be interested in a different future?" he asked after I had finished telling of my plans concerning the Lvov military-political school.

I shrugged my shoulders as if to say, "Let's hear about it and then we'll see."

"We know that you are organizer of the young Communists in your group. You are a good photographer. We are even aware that the captain of your ship wants to put you forward for the job of cypher clerk, which is the highest degree of trust that can be shown a sailor. You prepared for entry into the institute for international relations, and you speak English."

"Not very well," I interjected.

"You are a sportsman and ought not to lose your temper in a difficult situation," he went on, frowning a little as he listed my virtues. "You get along easily with people. You are inclined to take risks. And you didn't even decide to get married, which is a good thing. So Oleg, would you not like to think about working abroad?"

"I'll complete my service and education, and then I'll be ready," I replied thinking that they wanted to recruit me as an "illegal" spy.

Oleg Maximovich seemed to have read my thoughts when he responded with a smile, "You are not obliged to continue your education. You are already sufficiently prepared. Incidentally, we are not talking about work in intelligence."

"What then?"

"Well, you would simply have to live abroad and observe certain things. Simply live there, without any of the spying business."

To tell the truth, I really didn't understand anything. What good would it do *them* if I went to live somewhere abroad? And in what role would I live there? As Sailor Tumanov?

Despairing of understanding anything, I muttered, "But what will then happen to my entry into the military-political school?"

"That doesn't bother us. Let everything carry on. Enjoy your leave and then go to Lvov. Do as you wish. Our only request is that we continue our meetings and chats for as long as you are on leave. Agreed?"

In the course of that month we met some ten times—sometimes in the hotel and on occasion in a restaurant. Sergei was usually present at those meetings.

Oleg Maximovich always stressed that I ought to take more interest in life in the West. At times I even caught myself thinking that perhaps he was deliberately trying to persuade me of how awful it was to live in Russia and how good it was in the West. Judging from everything he said, he knew life in the West to the last detail.

Much later I understood why he did it and appreciated the delicate work of this counterintelligence officer. On one occasion he inquired about what I knew about the activities of the émigré anti-Soviet organizations. I tried to think. I seemed to have read something in the papers about them. The Soviet press usually used the most abusive language when writing about those organizations. But I couldn't think of anything more specific.

"All right, but let us suppose you end up in the West. How would you relate to those people, our former citizens, who have now sold themselves to the Voice of America, the BBC, or the radio station Svoboda?"

"I would spit in their faces," I said, wanting to demonstrate the level of my ideological and political training.

"That's great," Oleg Maximovich replied crossly. "You arrive in the West, also as an émigré. You have to live with them—and there are all sorts among them. They are not all enemies. They have to be studied and you have to work with them."

Disheartened, I remained silent and once again quite confused.

On leaving Oleg Maximovich handed me a large pile of articles and booklets containing information about Russian émigré organizations in Europe and overseas and told Sergei to bring another bundle of similar materials to our next meeting.

On another occasion the officer asked, "Do you know what the Constitution is?"

"Yes, I do."

"And what defense of the constitutional order means?"

"Well, that's what I do on my destroyer . . . "

"That's true, only we protect our regime in a variety of ways. We are surrounded by enemies. There are enemies everywhere. The last time I spoke to you about émigré organizations. There are lots of them—the NTS, the OUN [Ukranian nationalists], the Union of Fighters for the Liberation of Russia, Radio Svoboda. . . . These are the worst and they burn with hatred for everything Soviet. That means we must be on our guard. We must study the enemy, know his intentions in advance, and strike preemptive blows."

With that, Oleg Maximovich handed me the usual pile of boring books. That was the way I passed my entire leave—reading this "fascinating" literature.

At the beginning of July, having received the necessary documents from the ship and a very complimentary recommendation from the editor of *Strazh Baltiki*, I set off for Lvov and the military-political school. On arrival I left my things in the station luggage room before reporting to the school, which was situated next to an attractive park. As it was laid down, I reported to the commanding officer, "Sailor Tumanov reporting to sit for the entrance examination for the faculty of journalism."

I didn't really intend to sit for any examinations. I had a great aversion to being a military person. And, I had the feeling that fate would deal with the questions of my future very soon.

Only a few of the men taking the preparatory course were sailors—the majority were soldiers. We naval men kept to ourselves, referring to the soldiers as "big boots." I didn't intend to sit for the examination so I treated the place like a sanitarium. I dozed off during lectures and in the evenings, instead of working in the library, I hopped the fence and went off to wander around Lvov—even though students were strictly forbidden from going into town.

I soon got to know another sailor by the name of Valentin. Assigned to the Pacific fleet, he had also come to Lvov for the sole purpose of introducing some variety into the course of his four-year service aboard ship. Valentin and I started having fun together. After the evening roll-call we were over the fence and free as the wind. There was wine, beer, and girls to have fun with and no patrols in the town.

When we had spent all of our money, and sold some of my uniform, Valentin came up with a way to quickly get rich again. Valentin's scheme took into account the psychological state of naval officers out strolling with their ladies. One of us would approach such a couple, introduce himself, and then explain that he was short of the two or three rubles needed to get him to where he was doing his military service. What officer, especially with a lady on his arm, could refuse to help a poor sailor? It looked like a con job, and did us no honor, of course, but it served our purpose.

Our dissolute manner of life continued for quite a long time. By the time we became bored with it, the exams, for which were were not prepared, were just ahead of us. It was time to get away and return to our fleets. We had had enough.

"Let's go to the top man," I suggested, "and tell him frankly that we have changed our minds about entering the school and have decided to finish our military service. After all, they won't shoot us."

"They won't shoot us," my bosom buddy Valentin agreed, "that's true, but they can put us in the cooler for all the games we've played."

And who should interrupt our gloomy thoughts? I couldn't believe my eyes. The very same young secret policeman by the name of Sergei. In some mysterious way he had turned up in Lvov at the school, moreover wearing the uniform of a naval captain-lieutenant.

He called me aside and said, with his fingers to his lips, "Shsh. Bear in mind that I am an officer on the staff of the brigade in which you are serving and I have been sent especially to check up on how the Baltic sailors are doing on their examinations. You understand? Now to business. Sailor Tumanov has caused us a lot of trouble with his games in Lvov."

"What games?" I tried to put on a look of innocence.

"Especially your performances at the railway station," Sergei pressed on. "There's acting talent going to waste in you and your friend."

I relaxed my expression. There was no point in denying it.

"But we are pleased with you. You have again demonstrated that you don't lose your head in difficult situations. That's important."

I continued looking at Sergei in disbelief. Had the danger really passed? Apparently it had. It seemed clear that he had not come to Lvov to educate me.

"Now listen Oleg. They will throw you out of the school. You must realize that."

"I myself intended to get away from here . . . "

"You will, of course, receive the corresponding character reference and you will return to your ship with a rather tarnished reputation . . . "

"That's OK with me."

"It's actually very good in view of *our* future plans. Let's talk about those tomorrow. I will find you. During the night refresh your memory of your earlier meetings with Ivan Ivanovich, Oleg Maximovich and me. Recall what we talked about and what we are preparing you for."

He shook my hand in an especially friendly way, as if with an equal, and we parted until the next day.

The next day I at last learned what was ahead for me. It was all said in a matter-of-fact manner, without any highfalutin words or special instructions. It all fit with the general direction of my recruitment and I appreciated the approach.

Sergei asked me casually, "Well? What about living abroad?"

"That would be alright," I replied cautiously, determined not to ask any superfluous questions.

"Then pay close attention. In September your ship leaves for the Mediterranean. You will be hanging around there for a long time, more than a month. But on one occasion—and you must remember this very carefully—the destroyer will drop anchor not far from the border between Egypt and Libya, opposite the little town of Es-Salum. There you will leave the ship, get yourself to Libya, and give yourself up to the English or Americans. You will tell them that you have always dreamed of living in freedom and of life in the West. Curse the Soviet system. Well, you can work out what to say on your own.

"How you will leave the ship is something you will have to decide for yourself in the light of the actual situation. Bear in mind that nobody on the destroyer will have been let in on the secret. But don't make any mistakes. If you find yourself in the hands of the Egyptians they will immediately hand you back to us. Then there will be trouble."

"What then?"

"Then," he laughed, "for a certain time you will, of course, have to feed the fleas in solitary confinement as a traitor to your country. Later we will get you out. But it is much better not to be caught by them. Too much hope has been placed in you.

"Now listen again. In Libya try not to stay very long with the local people. That's also dangerous because we have an embassy there and they will surely demand that the Libyans hand you over. You must get out as quickly as possible to the West, settle down there, and establish contacts with émigré circles."

"But the English and Americans may want to ask me about my past. What should I tell them and what should be kept to myself."

"They *may* ask?" Sergei asked. "They'll drag the guts out of you with their questioning and they'll take months checking up on you, digging back to your grandmothers and grandfathers and all the girls you've ever been out with."

"And what should I tell them?" I asked, rather confused.

Sergei was obviously amused by my question. He was really enjoying it.

"Look here, Oleg. You have escaped from your ship because you want freedom and a lovely life in the West, is that right? You always wanted to see the world? You dreamed of it! We will go further. There is absolutely nothing in your background that would not please the people over there or prevent you from remaining in the West. You went to school. You fought against the hooligans. You failed to get into an institution. You worked in a Soviet enterprise. You took courses at the institute of foreign

relations. You served in the navy. About all of that—I repeat, all of it—
you can speak completely openly. About your parents. About your
friends. About your uncle who works in the KGB. About your service on
a destroyer. Don't conceal anything and don't try to deceive them. If they
catch you lying it will be bad for you. But there's no point in you lying.
Your trump card is your complete honesty. If they question you about
your work in the Yakovlev design bureau tell them about everything you
saw there—you don't know any secrets anyway. If they want detailed
information about your destroyer, tell them about it—the armament, the
names of the officers, the firing system. In a year's time the old bucket
will go for scrap."

"But won't all this be like real treachery?"

"That's just it!" The "captain-lieutenant" was even more pleased.
"That's exactly what we need from you—real treachery. We want a
perfect performance. You don't have to think up anything or conceal
anything. Just tell the truth. That's the only way we can achieve our aim."

"And what is the aim?"

"I repeat. Remain in any country in the West, settle down somewhere
among émigrés, and simply live life normally. For a year or two just live,
put down some roots, make some friends, and look around. Then, when
you feel that you are well established, write a letter to your parents
telling them how you are getting on. We will find you by that letter. You
will then have a meeting with someone you know. But don't bother about
that now, there's no need for the moment."

"What about my parents?"

"Nothing bad will happen to them. For appearance's sake they will be
summoned to the KGB for questioning and then sent home. After that we
will take care of them."

Sergei then adopted a more serious tone. "Try to erase just one thing
from your memory—your meetings with us. They never took place.
There were some KGB people involved in the operational unit, and here
you could mention Ivan Ivanovich as the man in charge. That's all. Full
stop. Nobody else. Forget everything. Wipe it out. Erase Oleg Maximovich and me from your past.

"If you finish up with with the Americans they are likely to want to
put you through a lie detector test! With that you only have to answer
'yes' or 'no.' The lie detector is. of course, unpleasant, but it can be
tricked. If they warn you about the test the day before, have a good night's
sleep that night and drink a glass of whisky or vodka the next morning.
Then no lie detector will frighten you. It's very simple, but effective."

Sergei gave a lot more advice of various kinds. He told me that if I had to get away from the ship by swimming not to be afraid of sharks because there were none there and that the water would be warm enough to allow me to reach the shore. He told me not to take anything with me. He asked me to cease all correspondence with relatives and friends from that day on. He said that, when the time came, they would find me, wherever I was on Earth. I simply had to write a letter to my parents.

Suddenly it struck me like an electric shock. "So it means that when I swim away from my ship it's for the rest of my life?"

"Why . . . " Sergei was at a loss to reply. "If it doesn't work out right over there, you will find a way of returning. But better if things do work out."

Toward the end of our conversation Sergei's voice gradually resumed a more official tone, reminding me that I was a candidate for membership in the Communist Party, that I was obliged to carry out my duty, and that *they* had faith in me.

"After all, you won't be alone there. There are many other fighters on that invisible front. Although nobody knows about them, they are there. They are fighting and the motherland will not forget their heroism."

I didn't really grasp the rest of what he was saying. The next day I was summoned to the head of the selection commission of the military-political school, and without any special explanation, dismissed from the course. They handed me a packet sealed with sealing wax, which I assumed contained my character reference and an account of all my sins. I was to hand the packet to my commander upon returning to my ship.

On the same day Valentin reported to the head of the selection commission with a request to be released. Strangely enough, he too was permitted to leave without any special problems. Our paths parted forever in Moscow. He took the Trans-Siberian railway to the Far East. I caught a train going west to Kaliningrad.

Man Overboard

By the middle of September our base in the Baltic was suddenly full of activity. The destroyer took on a supply of fuel, its ammunition store was replenished, and its hold was filled with macaroni, potatoes, tinned meat, sugar, coffee, and tea—in hitherto unheard of quantities. The old hands knew at once what it meant: We were going on a voyage that could take many months. Previously we had not left the limits of the Baltic.

I was probably the only person in the crew who knew where the Spravedlivy was going, but I said nothing.

An officer from the "special department" joined the ship at the base, which was also a sign that the ship would soon leave on a long voyage. (Employees of the so-called "special departments" in the Soviet Armed Forces were officers of the third directorate of the KGB and carried out counterintelligence functions.) The counterintelligence man wasted no time. He continually invited sailors who inspired confidence in him to his cabin for confidential talks, and, as it turned out, he chose me as a potential agent. He reminded me that I had been in the youth organization, was a candidate for membership in the party, and was therefore obliged to report anything suspicious to him.

"I will certainly inform you," I assured him.

Three days before we put out to sea the commander read the following order: "We are heading for the Mediterranean, where we will be part of a joint squadron of ships from three fleets—the Baltic, the Black Sea, and the Northern—to carry out our fighting task."

At that time the Soviet Navy was starting to adopt Admiral Gorshkov's doctrine, which called for a more active confrontation with the American Navy on the oceans of the world. Until then, the Yankees had been the absolute masters of the oceans, while our ships had kept close to the shore, never venturing far from their bases. Now, having gathered strength, the Soviet fleet had thrown out a challenge to the United States' armada of aircraft carriers and submarines.

The Mediterranean was one region where this confrontation was especially sharp and where the deadly dangerous game of cat and mouse never ceased for a moment.

It was in September 1965, I believe, that the Americans discovered for the first time that they were no longer the masters in that strategically important region. Our combined squadron—the cruiser *Sverdlov*, two destroyers, two submarines, and a floating dock—followed closely in the wake of the Americans' Sixth Fleet. As far as I could understand, our squadron's main task was to demonstrate our presence. In doing do, the Kremlin was shaking its fist at the White House and all others who dared to ignore the military might of the Soviet Union.

Judging by their behavior, I believe that the Americans were apparently worried by what was for them a new show of Soviet strength. Their Neptune reconnaissance planes were constantly overhead. The commanders of their ships were obviously nervous. Our people also felt very strained. As a result, some strange situations came about.

On one occasion, a buoy used to track submarines was dropped from an American aircraft. As luck would have it, it landed about one hundred and fifty meters from the side of our destroyer, prompting lively discussion on the bridge. Our commander immediately ordered the launch of a cutter, with his senior deputy at the wheel, to pick up the buoy. One of the officers expressed doubts: What if the thing was loaded with explosives? They would get near it and it would blow up. The senior deputy turned pale and looked hopefully at the commander. He wasn't anxious to risk his life.

Our commander was a man with a great vocabulary of swear words and a very determined sailor who, scorning all regulations, usually stood on the bridge in pants, undershirt, and hat. He berated the officer with some tough swear words and ordered him to carry out his orders.

The buoy was successfully lifted out of the water and delivered to the bridge. As someone with a knowledge of English, I was ordered to translate the writing on its side. It said: "Property of the Army of the USA."

"To hell with that," the commander commented as he shook his fist at the aircraft circling overhead. "It is now the property of the glorious Navy of the Soviet Union." To this statement, the commander added a long stream of unprintable phrases about the Americans—words that flattened the ears of even the most hardened seagoers.

Suddenly one of the radio operators came rushing out of the information office like a scalded cat. "Comrade commander, your voice is on the air and can be heard far away," he said.

The buoy had been equipped with hydrophones and had transmitted clearly to the world the whole of our discussion about it. In a fit of temper, the commander ordered that our prize be thrown overboard. After he had cooled down, however, he rescinded the order and instead had the buoy hidden in the deepest possible hold.

We were lying somewhere in the middle of the Mediterranean by the beginning of November. The commander gave the order: "The ship is to go for painting!" Why was this? No parades or inspections were planned. The more experienced older men suggested that we were going to put in to a foreign port—a rumor that excited all. What did a visit to a foreign port mean to a Soviet sailor? It was an adventure that would last a lifetime—a chance to come into contact, even for a day, with a world Russians knew only from books and newspapers. A world that Russian propaganda cursed in the most extreme language, but nevertheless drew every Communist toward it.

"If they let us go ashore," the veterans said, "we'll be able to buy souvenirs and get rich—lighters, ballpoint pens, and badges."

It was, of course, the stuff of dreams.

The deck of the *Spravedlivy* was covered with three coats of paint and every possible surface was swabbed down. Again, our anchor was raised and it appeared we were setting a course for Egypt.

"To Alexandria," whispered the experts excitedly. But I thought to myself, Egypt is not in my plans. Could something have changed?

As it turned out there was no need for alarm. All the fuss was explained by the fact that we were to carry out a series of combined exercises with the Egyptian Fleet and were going to invite the Egyptians aboard.

The next day we caught sight of their first ship. It was a destroyer built by the English in the 1930s, and it smoked so badly that you could tell where it was—even beyond the horizon. We gave our "friends" a warm welcome. A banquet was held aboard the cruiser *Sverdlov* for the officers, and the Egyptian sailors invited the crew of the *Spravedlivy* to join. The cook prepared a fine meal, and we were ordered to wear parade dress. The banquet did not, however, pass without incident. The main dish the cook prepared was made of tinned pork, and our guests categorically refused to eat it. No one had realized that offering a Moslem pork was a terrible insult. We had difficulty smoothing things over.

After our joint maneuvers were completed, the Egyptian destroyer took the lead toward Egypt. The shore was soon visible. We dropped anchor about three miles out, and I, taking advantage of my friendship with the navigation officer, immediately checked our position. We were opposite the land border between Egypt and Libya and the village of Es-Salum was visible. This was my departure site!

I was scared. It wasn't the business of escaping that worried me—I had long ago come to terms with that. I had developed something like courage and daring. The unknown excited me, causing adrenalin to pump through my veins. I was, however, frightened by the thought of the three miles between the destroyer and the shore. Although I was not a bad swimmer and could hold out for quite a long time in the water, I had never swum so far from land.

Again and again I measured myself up to the distance. It was obvious that I would have to swim at night. Could I reach the shore before dawn? What if they caught me before? They could sound the alarm and send a cutter after me. . . . As I was swimming, the Egyptians might alert their border guards and grab me as soon as my feet touched the ground. No, I didn't like the thought of those three miles.

Meanwhile, life went on as usual. Officers continued to exchange visits. Our commander presented the commander of the Egyptian destroyer with a beautiful model of the *Spravedlivy*. Some of the best craftsmen on the destroyer had worked long on it. Everything was made exactly to scale — every gun and every porthole. The model was placed in a specially made glass case with an appropriate engraved message. It was presented to the Egyptian commander with solemn ceremony. The commander naturally looked forward to receiving a present of similar "caliber" in return. Imagine his disappointment when the Egyptian officer handed him a cheap box made from papier mâché. Our gallant commander vented his feelings with very strong language.

Suddenly the whole group of ships raised anchor and made for the open sea. They started joint target practice. Whether we were to return, no one could say. I began cursing myself for not making up my mind, believing that I had missed my chance. But then, having demonstrated the frightening power of Soviet weaponry, the squadron turned around and by nighttime had again dropped anchor in the very same place. The good Lord must have been aware of my anxiety because in the morning our destroyer (why ours?) was ordered to weigh anchor again and move in closer to the shore. Now only about one mile separated us from land. You could hear the donkeys braying in Es-Salum.

My time had come. It was now or never.

I had been through the encyclopedia in the ship's library to see what it said about Libya. Then I carried out a "reconnaissance in action" — I asked the navigation officer when we would be going to Alexandria. (In fact, I wanted to know how long we were going to remain where we were.)

The officer kindly laid out the map and said, "We're not going to Alexandria. The day after tomorrow we leave here for good."

That meant I had two nights. I decided to make an attempt that very night. It was the eighteenth of November.

I tore up and quietly threw all my papers and letters overboard. I prepared a lightweight sports outfit, tennis shoes, a bottle of fresh water, and a few needles in case I got cramps in the water. The sea appeared to be quite warm, but you never knew.

In the evening I dropped my things overboard at the end of a rope, which was the way we did our laundry "illegally." The rope would be useful later, when I would use it to silently slide down into the water. I didn't plan to dive in from the deck.

The lights out signal sounded. I laid down in my hard bunk in the crew's quarters with the others and pretended to sleep. I needed to wait until two o'clock in the morning — a time when there would be no one on the bridge except a couple of signallers keeping watch. And, as I had learned on more than one occasion, the signallers were not especially vigilant at that time.

Only three days before I had celebrated my twenty-first birthday. At my age other Russians were studying at university, had found jobs, went dancing, attended weddings, drank cheap wine, took part in young Communist meetings, saved money to buy tape recorders, sang Vysotsky's songs, went on expeditions, read Solzhenitsyn, cursed American imperialism, dreamed of having American jeans, went to Siberia to work on the "great constructions of communism," and declaimed the poems of Yevtushenko—life was completely normal and agreeable to most. Neither they nor their parents (if they hadn't been born before 1917) knew any other life.

I was one of them, a typical young man in Moscow in the mid-1960s. No worse and no better than many others. I simply wanted to finish my military service, go back home, find a job that suited me, and marry a nice girl . . . but fate had decided differently. And very soon, I would break with, and in fact betray, my past. In carrying out my escape from the ship I was turning my back on everything that had been my life for twenty-one years. In Russia I would be declared a rotten traitor. A military court would probably sentence me to death. All my relatives and friends would be dragged in for interrogation by the KGB: some might have difficulties at their work or school "for having contact with a renegade." It was possible that no one would ever learn the truth about Oleg Tumanov.

Was it not too great a price to pay for my forthcoming adventure?

And what about my new life? How would it work out in a foreign land? What would happen to me in a day, a year, or even ten years? I realized how small my chances were of getting somewhere where I could be of some benefit to the KGB.

The darker the southern night became outside the porthole, the more alarmed I became. For the first time in months I felt an almost domestic comfort in the bare crew's quarters. Before they had seemed like a hated metal cage. Now, I suddenly caught myself envying the comrades I was leaving behind. As it came closer to two o'clock, I began to have a nervous tremor.

I certainly did not then resemble the super-agent James Bond.

Time to go! Still unable to control my nervousness, I stood up and put on the light sports outfit and tennis shoes. I remembered to pick up a cigarette and matches. If anyone approached me on deck I would say that I had come out for a smoke. That was not forbidden.

The night was quiet and warm. The big southern stars were bright enough to prevent me from getting lost on the way to the land.

I inhaled greedily on the cigarette, putting off the moment of decision. Stepping carefully, I went to the place where the rope was hanging from the deck. I stood still and listened. No, there was nothing to interfere with my plan. It was time . . .

As I shimmied down the rope into the water, my foot caught on one of the portholes. Something fell somewhere inside the ship. I froze. But nobody woke up. Nobody raised the alarm. Fortune smiled on me that night.

Once in the sea, I dived down, trying to swim under water as far as possible from the ship. Gradually, as the distance between me and the destroyer increased, my self-confidence returned. There was no way back. I had made my choice.

To reserve my strength and not get out of breath I approached the shore quietly. There was only one incident that made my heart beat faster. At about the half-way point I heard the engine of a motor boat approaching. Were they after me? I looked around. Nobody was pursuing me, but the sound of the motor was nevertheless getting louder. When I saw the boat was quite close I took as much air into my lungs as I could and dived. There was, however, no real reason for alarm. The motor boat was from the cruiser *Sverdlov* and was obviously attending to business that had nothing to do with me. Perhaps it was officers returning after one of their regular parties with the Egyptians.

At last my feet touched the pebbles of the shore. I had reached dry land. I took a brief rest, removed and wrung out my clothing, threw away the needles that were no longer needed, and began to look around. The flask of fresh water was lost, but my watch was in good working order.

I now needed protection from the early morning cold. My wet clothes stuck to my body, and although my anxiety had passed, my teeth chattered. I determined where the border between Egypt and Libya was and set off in that direction at a good pace, keeping in mind that it was dangerous for me to hang around in Egypt.

Although the area was hilly, there were no special obstacles to impede my progress. I stopped only at sunrise. It seemed to me that I had already covered a tremendous distance. Imagine my disappointment when I looked back and saw that the destroyer and cruiser were still quite close. But I appeared to have crossed the border and for that reason felt myself to be in greater safety. In a narrow gully I picked a smooth rock that the sun had warmed, laid down on it, and went to sleep.

A couple of hours later, rested and dry, I walked into Libyan territory. I knew that there was only one road along the coast that links Egypt and

Libya that could lead me to an inhabited place. I now had to find it.

It was near midday when I met a camp of Bedouin shepherds at the top of a hill. They gave me strong tea, treated me to macaroni with tomato sauce, and directed me to the main road.

"English?" they asked.

"English," I replied. All other communications between us took place with the aid of gestures.

Toward evening, when I had covered enough distance to lose sight of the sea, I met another shepherd with a small flock of sheep. He knew a few words of English, so we were able to have a fairly meaningful conversation. The shepherd gave the wandering "Englishman" a good meal and made up a bed for him with a good coverlet. Then he settled himself down nearby and played his pipes for a long time. In the morning I felt so moved by his warm hospitality that I gave him my watch—the only item of value I had.

Well rested, I soon reached the main road and came across a signpost that said it was a little more than one hundred kilometers to the town of Tobruk. I rejoiced: Sergei had talked to me about Tobruk. I had seen it on maps—everything was going right.

I got a lift in a Land Rover and arrived at the first military post with a telephone. It was time to hand myself over as a prisoner. I explained to the Libyan officer in English—with some difficulty—who I was and where I came from. After hearing me out he nodded and said, "Since you have fallen off a Soviet ship, you should go to Cairo."

"I didn't fall, I left my ship myself. I ran away, do you understand?"

"All the same you had better go to Cairo." He repeated the name of the Egyptian capital several times, "Cairo, Cairo, Cairo . . ."

Oh dear, I thought, now he will hand me over to the Egyptians and that will be the end of the expedition. I called up the whole of my vocabulary and tried to get it into the officer's head that I needed urgently to get to the Americans or the English. Only to them and nobody else. The Libyan left to use the telephone. They fed me and gave me a couple of packs of cigarettes. Then they transported me to the hinterland in a military Jeep.

That night we stopped in a little town beyond Tobruk and I had a very pleasant surprise. Despite the late hour, they took me to a local shop and bought me new clothes. After changing my rags, I looked at myself in the mirror: only the three-day growth of my beard remained to remind me of my escape from the ship.

My week in the military settlement near Benghazi passed fairly uneventfully. Some Libyans turned up to whom I repeated the same story over and over again. Three bodyguards were always at my heels.

But my hosts treated me politely, fed me in an agreeable European restaurant and, so that I would not be bored, gave me a transistor radio. But where were the Americans or the English? Surely they were not going to send me to Cairo after all?

At last, when I had almost reconciled myself to that thought, some new people—from the British Embassy—arrived in the little town. With them was a female interpreter who spoke quite tolerable Russian. I now had the possibility of explaining properly who I was and what I wanted.

"Soviet sailor, Oleg Tumanov. Escaped from the destroyer *Spravedlivy* because I want to live in the West. Yes, I left voluntarily. Yes, I do not like the Communist regime. No, I have not changed my mind . . ."

They asked me lots more questions of the same kind and afterwards asked me if I had any problems or requests. Requests? I asked them again to help me obtain permission to live in England or in any other country in the West. With that the visitors departed.

From that day on they visited me regularly. The female interpreter was replaced with a former Soviet citizen who had been living in North Africa since the second World War. A month later a ginger-haired gentleman arrived: he turned out to be the military attaché in the British embassy.

"Be ready to move from here tomorrow," he said. "And, so that there won't be any problems with the Libyans we will tell them that we are inviting you to come hunting with us. You understand—hunting."

There were no problems. Outside the territory of the military settlement another car, containing a British interpreter, awaited us. We set off in the direction of Tobruk.

"I hope we are not going to Egypt?"

"Forget about Egypt," said the ginger-haired one with a laugh when he noticed my concern. "We are going to the British Air Force base. They have already been sniffing around about you at the Soviet embassy in Tripoli and are demanding that you be handed over. It is dangerous for you to stay here any longer."

Later I learned that the Soviet naval command had put a great deal of pressure on the Libyan authorities to hand me over. They even invented a story that I had killed a sailor on watch during my escape. That meant that they were insisting on the return, not simply of a sailor who had escaped, but of a serious criminal. I would be interesting to know if that "canard" had been approved by the KGB. I fear that it had not. If not, it meant that they had clearly gone too far, because my "legend" did not foresee anything like that. Actually, neither the British nor the Americans believed the story of the "murder."

All of the other maneuvers performed in Russia after my escape were done faultlessly. The truth about Tumanov was only known by three or four people: All the rest were convinced of my treachery. The investigation machine worked at full steam.

Twenty years later my childhood friend, Tolik Yesiava, who was by then the head of a major building trust, would recount the fuss my escape from the ship evoked.

In November 1965, he, then a soldier, was summoned by a representative from counterintelligence. Apart from the intelligence officer, whom he knew, there were two officers in naval uniform in the room. They questioned Tolya about everything connected with our friendship, only explaining after two hours of interrogation — and then unwillingly, with clenched teeth — that their curiosity was the result of my sudden disappearance. According to Yesiava, he told the intelligence officers in no uncertain terms that he totally disbelieved the story that I had jumped ship.

"It could only have been an accident," he told them.

Tolya was questioned from morning to late at night. An officer was sent to the barracks to search his belongings, and took away the letters I had written to my friend. They were interested in the tiniest details of my life story, my habits, aspects of my character, and my circle of friends and acquaintances. An officer from the special department had two more talks with him to clear up some details.

Tolya was summoned to the local KGB office. They got him to listen to a recording of a "Liberty" program in which a certain Shulgin was taking part.

"Do you recognize the voice?"

"Yes," replied my disheartened friend. "Only that's not Shulgin. It's Oleg Tumanov."

"Could you write a letter to Tumanov?" they asked Tolya.

"Of course."

"But perhaps it would be better for the letter to be written by Tatyana Bavykina?"

I had had an affair with Tatyana and the KGB man apparently wanted to catch the defector on the hook of love.

Tolya agreed, "Yes, if she writes it will probably be more agreeable for Oleg."

Tolya was never questioned again, however, and nobody was ever asked to write any letters.

Tolya Yesiava told me that when I first disappeared, and later when I appeared on Radio Svoboda, he was greatly puzzled. He couldn't believe that I was a traitor. In his own mind he decided: "Oleg certainly was given some task by the intelligence service, and the KGB is deliberately confusing the situation to mislead hostile questioning if they go after him." Well, he wasn't far from wrong. They even interrogated my parents. Tolya visited them several times and recalled how bitterly upset my mother was, thinking that she had lost her son forever. My father behaved with more restraint. Tolya reckons that my father may have guessed, or even that he had been told the truth, about the real reasons for my long absence.

Whatever the truth was, I find it painful to think about that time and what my parents had to live through.

But let me return to Libya and my journey with the British to their airbase.

During the Second World War, North Africa was the arena for the most furious battles between the fascists and the Allies. As I walked through the deserted hills I saw evidence of the battles that had taken place: piles of rusted shell cases, collapsing trenches, and pieces of barbed wire. Along our route we came across old military cemeteries—British, Italian, and German. The military attaché stopped and laid flowers on the graves of his countrymen.

After we had passed that sad place we stopped by the side of the road for a picnic. The Englishmen set out food on the grass and opened bottles of mineral water. Suddenly the expression on the military attaché's face froze, as though he had seen a poisonous snake approaching. What was the matter?

"Look," he said, pointing to the black car that had just swept past us, "That's a Volga from the Russian embassy. What is it doing down here?"

The picnic ended. The provisions were loaded in the car and we continued on our way.

Before we drove into the El-Adam airbase the interpreter drew my attention to old guns mounted on each side of the gateway.

"Do you recognize them?"

I shrugged my shoulders. "No."

"They are the 45-millimeter anti-tank guns that the Germans captured from the Soviets before Moscow and transferred here to use against us."

I spent less than a day at the base, where the Vulcan strategic bombers were stationed. I had the great pleasure of taking a bath: there had been no water in the Libyan village and even washing one's hands had been a problem. I had an evening meal with the general commanding the base. I appreciated the comfort with which the English had managed to arrange their life in the middle of a barren desert. I even received an unexpected gift from the general—a suitcase and a real English sweater, which later served me for many years.

I was received with respect and understanding, but not excessive curiosity.

I was discovering for myself an absolutely new world in which everything, literally everything, differed from our ways. It wasn't particularly difficult to learn to use shampoo or to distinguish between brands of cigarettes, but it was much more difficult to understand the system of human values and the moral and legal coordinates that were accepted in the West. I still had to get used to and understand Western ways: I would make many mistakes and miscalculations and sometimes hurt myself in the process.

Apart from the understandable difficulties the new life concealed in itself, there were a mass of fascinating revelations. Take, for instance, the part of Russian culture that censorship had hidden from Soviet citizens. Books by Nabokov and Pasternak, and poems by Solzhenitsyn and Galich, all were now accessible to me, exactly as they were to everyone else in the West.

I was not shy, and I had sufficient energy to greedily absorb everything new and unfamiliar. I did not hesitate to ask the people around me about anything I did not understand, and within three or four months I had gotten the feel of things well enough not to think much about Moscow. Gradually, toward the end of the first year, I became a typical Russian émigré in the West.

On the morning after our arrival at the airbase the interpreter came to me very concerned.

"Oleg, the situation has taken an unexpected change for the worse."

"Not Cairo, after all?" I thought to myself with some fright.

"The thing is, the British Foreign Secretary is planning a visit to the Soviet Union, and London wants to avoid any complications with the Kremlin. You understand? Your embassy in Tripoli has already made it known that they know you are at the El-Adam base and is demanding a meeting with you."

I indicated that I would reject such a meeting: my plans did not provide for such a thing.

"Then," the interpreter continued, "it would be better for you to leave here as soon as possible."

"I have no objections."

"But there is a snag. We cannot transport you into British territory."

So maybe that have decided to send me to South America or Australia, I thought.

"But we English have faithful allies in the form of the United States of America. And they have in principle nothing to worry about. They can take you in. If, of course, you agree to that."

"I'm agreeable," I said, perhaps a little too quickly and too eagerly.

"Fine then," the interpreter was delighted, as though he had so far been afraid that I might refuse. "The American plane is already here. We must hurry."

The general himself accompanied me to the aircraft and before take-off I thanked him sincerely (and in his person Her Majesty the Queen of Great Britain) for the hospitality I had been shown. It would have been very wrong of me not to have paid my respects to the English. After the Libyans, they had taken me in, cared for me, supported me, and had not let me get lost.

A flight to Greece in an ancient two-engined Dakota, then an immediate transfer to a big jet-powered aircraft full of electronic equipment and—oranges. A night landing at Frankfurt-on-Main. A fresh interpreter. He introduced himself as Alex and he would become part of my life for many months to come. I learned later that Alex was a colonel in the American military intelligence.

On December 5, 1965, I entered the territory of West Germany, never thinking that I was now in the country that would be my home for the next twenty years.

The Lie Detector Doesn't Work

I am a fatalist. I believe in fate. As it is written at your birth, so it will be. But that does not prevent me from looking back, analyzing my past, and trying to figure out why things happened in the way they did. I have reflected a great deal about why the KGB selected me for their purposes and have come to the following conclusions. They were sizing up the more intelligent lads in the young Communist operational unit, looking for the ones who might be used in security work. They would later recommend certain ones for counterintelligence, and others for the thankless task of pursuing dissidents. The most difficult of all for them was the selection of people for specific tasks in the West. Here it was apparent that the state security spared neither time nor effort. If you reconstruct the whole chain of events (as I have tried to do) it is clear that the security people had been "leading" me to Munich ever since my school days.

First they studied me in depth. Of course, from the very beginning they were attracted to me because all of my close relatives, apart from my brother, were connected to the KGB. I have already spoken about my mother and father. My uncle—the husband of my mother's sister—reached the rank of general in the government personal security service. My father's closest friend was a military attaché in Canada. All this not only simplified the business of checking up, but also guaranteed any future operation against unforeseen leaks. The old KGB employees, especially those who joined the service in Stalin's day, knew how to hold their tongues.

So my relatives and their friends may, without knowing it, have played an important role in my fate.

The check-up was carried out in all directions at the same time, including the detailed medical examination. Moreover, it was done in such a way that at no point did I feel I was tied to the KGB. And that was very reasonable, bearing in mind that I might expect to be subjected to very serious "X-rays" by Western counterintelligence services.

For some reason I went through the medical examination as a candidate for the institute of civil aviation. It was a very exacting process, but the special services obtained the most detailed information about my state of health, including the results of tests of my psychological stability. That information apparently satisfied them, and as a result the construction of my "legend" went ahead according to a set scheme from which there were no deviation.

For a job they deliberately offered me the Yakovlev design bureau. It was easier to keep an eye on me in that government enterprise, and what's more, it would make it more difficult for the special services of the West to check up on me later because entering a well-guarded territory and obtaining access to documents would be nearly impossible. Again, they probably reasoned that the "defector Tumanov" would, if he wished, be able to raise his price by telling the West about a secret Moscow enterprise, and it was very highly classified information.

The courses at the international relations institute also had a certain logic. Where, if not there, could a working lad acquire a foreign language in a year and a half and gain some elementary knowledge about life abroad? That too they had thought up quite well.

Even my improvisation over entering the military-political school fit well in the "legend" they so carefully created. According to the legend a young man without any precise purpose in life had escaped to the West. He was a fairly adventurous person, an extreme individualist, non-political, and inclined to make unexpected and unpredictable moves.

As a matter of fact, that is almost what I was in reality. I didn't need to pretend very much, to put on an act, or to invent things. In that sense the KGB scenario could not have been better written.

On the ship I had been accepted as a candidate for membership in the Communist Party of the Soviet Union, but, to tell the truth, I did not make the slightest effort to make that connection. It is possible that the political officer picked me out because of my skill with photography and my ability to write reports for the fleet newspaper—although that was not a display of "Communist political sense" but of a selfish desire to make my military service easier.

Nobody tried to force me to be a spy. I was not subjected to blackmail or other pressures, and there were no attempts to bribe me with material goods. For my part, it was a case of sober calculation magnified by a youthful desire for adventure. The taste for adventure was clearly part of my nature. And the calculation? To spend some time abroad in the risky role of an illegal intelligence agent meant getting myself out of the joyless Soviet society, to see the world and experience new emotions. That game was worth the risks.

"Let's get to know each other. They call me Sam, just Sam. I'll be working with you for some time."

The little stooped man in a hat and raincoat, looking like a typical minor official, walked confidently into the house, took off his coat and, like a host, sat down at the table and invited me to take the seat opposite him. He had a withered arm—I sensed it when we shook hands—and cold eyes. And he was very businesslike and unemotional. Sam talked only about what interested him.

He was interested in naval cyphers and shipboard communications systems. I told him that I would be glad to help him, but didn't know anything about the subject. About the organization of the artillery—gladly—that was where I served and I was like a fish in water on that subject. But cyphers . . . I tried once again to make him realize that I didn't know about cyphers and it was useless to waste time on that.

"Never mind," said Sam calmly. "Perhaps you will manage to remember something."

"How can I remember something I never knew?"

"You are making a mistake, Mister Tumanov. Of course you know. Tell me the name and rank of your cypher clerk."

I strained my memory. "Petty officer so-and-so, but I can't recall his name," I said.

"Show me the place on the destroyer where his quarters were situated. So now tell me how often the cypher clerk went to the commander with documents. Very good! And you say you know nothing. You know a great deal, Mr. Tumanov, and that is why I hope our meetings will continue."

At that time all refugees from the Soviet Union and the countries of Eastern Europe were screened in the West German camp at Zirndorf. I was dealt with by the American military intelligence at Camp King. On the one hand, I was fortunate, because the Americans provided their "clients" with extremely comfortable living conditions and paid them a weekly stipend. On the other hand, however, the screening there was much more severe. They spent six months "cleaning me out" in Frankfurt, and Sam, who I later learned was a bigwig at the CIA headquarters in Langley, was one of the inquisitors. While I was undergoing my screening, I was also undergoing exhausting interrogations concerning my presence in the Mediterranean and service in the Soviet navy in general.

For the second time the bigwig took me aback with a question: "And where did you hide what you brought with you from the ship?"

I stared at him in amazement.

"Mister Tumanov, you are an intelligent person. When you were planning your escape you must have provided yourself with a few secrets. Perhaps some documents, some maps or plans. . . . Where did you hide them? Under what rock in Libya? Just tell us where and we will find them."

He continued to question me like that for a long time. Then he finally gave up and disappeared back to Washington. My next questioner was also from the United States. He was an American of Russian origin named Boris. He brought me a present of caviar. Boris was interested in my work at the Yakovlev design bureau, in particular everything connected with what was then a new aircraft, the Yakovlev 28. Boris recorded all of our conversations on a Dictaphone.

"Try to remember where its fuel tanks were," he kept on with his tedious questions. "What sort of wing mechanism did it have? What do you know about its armament?" Finally I appealed to him: "Aren't you asking too much of an apprentice draftsman?" Remembering the instructions I had received in Moscow, I told them everything I could, but I fear the Americans regarded it as childish prattle.

It was easier to work with Boris for the simple reason that he regularly lubricated his throat with a glass or two of whiskey. He did not make himself out to be a bigwig—he would ask me to supper with him and once we even went to the cinema together.

Next came two Englishmen who questioned me about the ship. The meetings with them did not take place in the apartment where I lived but

in another one that had a German housekeeper. The principal Englishman amazed me by his slovenly appearance—his shirt was torn, his
jacket was shiny from age, and the housekeeper handed him his mackin-
tosh with two fingers for fear of getting dirty. The Englishmen inquired
politely about the arrangement of the ship, its armament, the firing
system, and the names of officers. On one occasion they showed me a
detailed plan of a destroyer of the same class as the *Spravedlivy*, from
which I concluded that these fellows knew a good deal more than I did.

The Americans allowed people from the West German intelligence
service (the BHD) to meet me only once. The Germans asked whether the
Soviet navy had any special plans with regard to West Germany. Alex
quickly got rid of them. I noted that he behaved very unceremoniously
with the Germans.

I later learned that Alex had the rank of colonel and worked in the
military intelligence in the "Soviet direction." A Pole by origin, he was
married to a Russian. I soon realized that, to a great extent, my future
depended on Alex. Not once did he give me the impression that he eyed
me with suspicion or distrust: on the contrary, his trump card was his
cordiality and goodwill. Dark-haired, rather thin, of medium height,
and smartly turned out, that was Alex. He met with me practically every
day, handing me a hundred Marks every week "for food." Coffee, cigarettes, and shampoo were issued as a separate ration. "All the German
stuff is rubbish," said Alex, and he knew what he was talking about.

The first apartment he put me in had two beautifully furnished rooms
and was situated not far from Frankfurt's main railway station. I found
the refrigerator full of all sorts of tasty foods and drinks, most of which I
had never seen before. A pile of Soviet newspapers and magazines were
laid on a little table in the bedroom. In the evening when I was left alone,
I made myself a luxurious scrambled egg, tried Coca-Cola for the first
time, and smoked my first Phillip Morris cigarette. Also, for the first
time in many days, I went to bed without a visible bodyguard.

It was not a bad beginning for my new life.

The next morning Alex brought a photographer who took front and
side pictures of me. The colonel then warned me that, beginning the next
day, a variety of people would visit and begin asking questions. He said
that I was always to tell the truth, because my every word would be
carefully checked.

"Remember, Oleg," Alex advised, "what happens to you in the future
will depend a great deal on how you answer questions now."

Three days later he asked me to carefully complete a pile of forms,
saying that they were necessary for drawing up the documents that

would give me the right to live in Germany. When he took the forms away, he gave me a card in a plastic holder on which was written in English that the owner was an employee of the United States Air Force. The card bore a Finnish name.

"Don't worry," Alex reassured me when he saw my surprise, "you won't be a Finn for long. It's the safest way, because there are very few people here who speak Finnish."

As I strolled the streets not far from the Kaiserstrasse one evening, I came across the nightclub district. Judging by the hoards of people, I surmised that there were bars and striptease joints. In those days, no Soviet would ever dare go anywhere near such establishments. But I was no longer a Soviet; I had a pass with a Finnish surname, and one hundred Marks in my pocket. Maybe I could risk it?

Forbidden fruit is always sweeter. In Russia, the Bolshevik system had been trying to forge the "new man"—a man of high moral qualities and pure in all aspects—for decades. But no sooner did that "new man" reach the West than he immediately began to take an interest in pornography. But he couldn't buy any magazine that struck his fancy because he had no money and was afraid of this fellow countryman: if they informed on him he would certainly be in trouble.

So I decided to go in. I would probably have to buy some drink. Would my hundred Marks be enough? I had already gotten to know the price of spirits in the shops. A bottle of good brandy cost eighteen Marks. Even if it was double the price in a nightclub I had more than enough to pay my way. Moreover, I wasn't going to buy a bottle. I would make do with a couple of glasses.

Dressed in the new suit Alex had brought, and a white shirt with a tie received through American aid to refugees, I set out for a nightclub. Right off, I had to pay ten Marks to leave my overcoat in the cloakroom. That put me on my guard. Nonetheless, I sat down at a little table and pointed to a bottle of brandy that was exactly the same as the one that cost eighteen Marks in the shops. I sat there, looking around me and sipping the brandy. Fine! A girl immediately perched herself by my side, muttered something in German, and, having discovered that I was a Finn, asked the "gentleman from Helsinki" to treat her to some champagne. I ordered a Picollo for her and another brandy for myself. I thought, "I'll take the girl back to my apartment." Since I was no longer watching the striptease show, I asked the bartender for my bill. He put the bill down on the table and what did I see? A hundred and thirty-five Marks! For what? For two glasses of brandy and a glass of bad champagne?

I had enough sense not to make a fuss. I simply took off the watch I had bought the day before and placed in on top of my hundred-Mark note. The bartender pushed the watch aside scornfully and spoke just one word: "Pay."

The girl had vanished and from somewhere in the darkness I could see a powerful thug of a man approaching, eyeing me suspiciously. "You are in a bad spot, runaway Tumanov," I thought. "You are going to get beaten up."

For some reason I pulled the card with the Finnish name on it out of my breast pocket. It gave the telephone number of the duty officer at the American base to which I was supposed to belong. To my surprise, at the sight of the card the aggressive ardor of the restaurant staff subsided. I later learned that owners of these types of establishments are terribly afraid of getting into confrontations with the Americans because insulting Yankees could lead to the loss of an operating license and other unpleasantness. So I had been right to use my "phoney" documents.

The bartender took the card and went to telephone. Half an hour later Alex, sleepy and bad tempered, arrived. He had apparently been awoken from his bed. Without a word, he paid the bartender the remainder of my bill and took me home. It was only when we reached my fourth-floor apartment that Alex vented his anger. He was especially surprised that I had intended to invite the tart from the nightclub to a clandestine apartment that belonged to United States military intelligence.

"If you had ended up with the police with a false document the Germans would have made a big fuss. You never would have been permitted to stay in Germany. I warn you, one more incident like that and we'll hand you over to the local authorities and let them decide your fate."

I remained silent.

I don't know whether it was because of this incident or for some other reason, but two days later I was moved to an apartment that was further away from the haunts of vice.

Alex, whose anger had by then cooled, said, "If you need a woman, just ask me. We will cover the expenses and deliver her to you here."

"I'll manage somehow," I said.

In the meantime, the screening process continued. Alex brought a detailed map of Moscow and tested my knowledge of the city. How do you get from this street to that one? What is the best form of transportation to use here? He asked me to draw a plan of the courtyard where I had lived and to indicate the entrances and how many seats were in the courtyard shelter. What was the name of the teacher you had in the first grade? Who was your instructor in shooting? What was the telephone number of your girlfriend? Name all of the officers who taught at the study center, and make a written list of all the young people who belonged to the operational unit . . . Alex wore me out with his inexhaustible curiosity. He drew the general picture, and when there was a need for greater precision he called in more "narrow" specialists.

When he learned that my uncle, Colonel Malofeyev, worked for the KGB and occasionally travelled abroad on business he immediately called in a man with a suitcase full of photographs. Details of visiting soccer teams from Moscow made to West Germany in the late 1950s were written on some of the pictures. My uncle — with the pretense of being a sports official — was a member of that delegation. I had no difficulty pointing him out in several pictures. The Americans were very pleased.

On another occasion a man turned up with photographs of the courtyard where I lived in Moscow. I was stupefied. There was my mother with her string bag dragging herself along after shopping, aged and sad. And there was my father coming out of the building's entrance. Our neighbors were standing around gossiping by the shelter. Children were playing. It made my heart ache to see such family pictures.

"Do you recognize anyone in these pictures? Which one? Show us and give their names."

Once they produced a photograph of an officer from our destroyer, apparently taken from a low-flying aircraft. Do you recognize him? Of course I did.

Yes, screening by the Americans was carried out in a very thorough manner. They did it seriously and conscientiously, without hurrying. But I wasn't in any hurry either. My whole life lay ahead.

When Alex's second daughter was born he celebrated by inviting me to have supper with him in a Chinese restaurant. He appeared with a bottle of champagne in one hand and a bundle of strange newspapers in the other on that day. He handed the papers to me.

"Have a look at these copies of *Posev*. It is published here by the same sort of Russians as you — émigrés."

The newspapers made a very strong impression on me. If I had been caught reading *Posev* in Moscow I would almost certainly have been thrown into prison. Every article was a scathing exposure of the "criminal essence of the Soviet regime." Such articles were not to be found even in the most hostile German and English newspapers. On seeing that *Posev* greatly interested me, Alex suggested that we go to a place "where there were masses of similar stuff" the next day. And so the next day I found myself in one of the rooms at the library of the American military township, lost in the world of the Russian-language émigré press and writings.

Before that day, I had looked at our (and my) life in the Soviet Union through the rose-colored glasses of Soviet propaganda. A person looking through those spectacles saw a myth that had been skillfully constructed in the Kremlin, rather than real life. We were characters out of a colossal historical miracle play, participants in a universal hypnotic seance.

I do not want to imply that everything in the Soviet Union was bad. I only mean to discuss the advantages and shortcomings of one system compared with the other. I am talking about the stifling lack of intellectual freedom—a feature of all totalitarian regimes. I am referring to the atmosphere of the lie that surrounds every citizen, which George Orwell described with such convincing force in his famous novel *1984*.

I now had the possibility of seeing life without ideological blinkers.

I noted the address of *Posev*'s editorial office and determined that I would get to know the people who had devoted their lives to fighting communism. I had no desire to join them, but was curious about the group and secretly hoped to build contacts that might be useful at a later time. I felt neither love nor hate for these people.

I telephoned *Posev*'s office, obtained an invitation to visit, and then took a taxi to a building surrounded with barbed wire. When I rang the bell, a watchman appeared, drove off a guard dog, and took me inside. It was, apparently, the store of the *Posev* publishing house, a branch of the National Labor Union—the NTS. In a big, poorly equipped room, at a long table on which old tins served as ashtrays, sat a rather fat man. It was apparent that he was expecting me.

"It was you who phoned? Where are you from?"

"From the Soviet Union."

"You are living with the Americans, aren't you?"

I confirmed his statement.

"Where is your apartment? What is your address?"

"That's of no importance," I said, now on my guard. "I live . . . "

The fat man didn't take offense. To the contrary, he treated me with confidence.

"Don't worry. We have good relations with the Americans and already know a lot about you. If you want to buy some books, please do. They are cheaper here than in the shops. Choose what you want. Incidentally, we had a visit a few days ago from another young man who has also just escaped from Russia. Would you like his address? He lives on Mozart Street. His name is Vladimir Krysanov."

The fat man gave me a couple of magazines, advised me not to lose touch with the NTS, and led me to the door. I later discovered that he was Artemov, one of the NTS leaders. Our relationship developed so well that Artemov eventually offered me a job in *Posev*'s publishing house, and the children of NTS officials who were of my age came to use our apartment as an evening meeting place—a sort of Russian youth club.

I say *our* apartment because the young man Artemov spoke of, Volodya, or Vladimir, Krysanov, soon became my roommate. Volodya was from Siberia. He was not very tall, had fiery red hair, and, like my brother, had graduated from the geology school of Moscow University. He had come to hate the Soviet regime and decided to go West, no matter what the cost. He managed to cross the Soviet-Finnish border and hitchhike to Sweden, where he gave himself up to the authorities. The Swedes handed him over to American military intelligence.

Alex had also been in charge of Volodya. It is curious that when we first met, Alex introduced himself to me as Lane; he introduced himself to Volodya as Lincoln. When I met Volodya he had already been "cleaned out" and screened and was awaiting permission to go the United States, where he intended to start his own business. Alex blessed our friendship, and in March 1966, moved us into a four-room apartment, located in the territory of the American military township in the northern part of Frankfurt.

It was at about that time that Alex delivered to me a document that gave me the right to live in Western Germany. It was called a "Fremdenpass"—the most simple passport for émigrés. I was nonetheless pleased to have it because it meant that my screening was coming to an end and that, so far, everything was going well.

"Soon we will get you a better document," Alex promised. He kept his word.

Sometime in the spring, Alex warned me that visitors from Munich were coming to see me the next day. He advised me to do everything I could to make a good impression. That was how I came to have my first meeting with people from the radio station Svoboda. George Perry and Edward Neimanis were from the audience research department of the station. When they came, they brought with them recorded tapes and transcribed texts.

"We would like to have your opinion about all this," George Perry explained. "Listen to the tapes, read the texts, and then give the interviewer your assessment of the program. You are recently from the Soviet Union, and so we can rely on you as a typical young listener. You will receive a fee for doing this." With that, he handed me some sheets of paper with a great many questions.

The new acquaintances I made that day were far more important than the two hundred Marks I received for the review. Volodya Krysanov, as a more experienced arrival in the West and my adviser, assured me, "Working for Svoboda is a lot better than having some job in the NTS printing shop."

"Yes, that would be a very interesting job," I burst out carelessly and then immediately bit my tongue. Plans for a future in the West were better concealed.

During that time I had other meetings with my former countrymen. On one occasion an Azerbaidjanian named Tofik, a sailor from the fishing fleet, invited Volodya and me to go fishing. Tofik had jumped ship in Hamburg the year before, and had apparently been affected mentally because he had a suspicious nature. He imagined that there were agents of the special services all around him—both local and Soviet. Even in his official American apartment Tofik frequently put his finger to his lips as if to say, "quiet, we're being bugged." He was sure that the whole apartment was full of hidden cameras and microphones.

"I have prodded all the walls in search of those spying things," Tofik complained, "and even though I've found nothing, I know for sure that they are watching me, even when I am sitting on the toilet."

"He's a schizophrenic," Alex told me when he learned of this new friend. And then he categorically forbade me to meet him again.

The next acquaintance I made was Victor Shishelyakin, a former soldier who, in 1962, had deserted from the group of Soviet troops in Germany. Victor was in the habit of strutting about year round in a suit, tie, and leather gloves (he never removed the leather gloves). He apparently imagined that his manner of dress was very chic. A former farm laborer from Siberia, Victor Shishelyakin was very homesick and constantly made tearful requests at the Soviet missions for permission to return to Russia. He would tell of how he had found the Soviet military mission in West Berlin and fallen on his knees before the general, saying, "I admit my mistake and I want to go home," and how the general had gloated over him, saying, "So it's you, the vile traitor Shishelyakin! You want to go home? You have to serve your country. You will crawl on all fours from Berlin to Brest."

"I would crawl," the repentant deserter would sigh mournfully, wiping aside a tear with his leather glove.

To earn forgiveness, Victor Shishelyakin used to wash the floors of the German-Soviet friendship club for nothing. Curiously, Alex, who was very well informed about all this, had no objection to our meeting Victor.

By April, matters connected with my screening seemed to be quite forgotten. They now rarely had talks with me. No new faces appeared, and I had the feeling that the process was coming to an end. In an attempt to relieve some of the monotony in our life, people in the NTS introduced us to a former Soviet German, Johann Weimer, who had only recently arrived back in his "historical motherland." During the Second World War, Johann and his family, who were from the Volga region, had been exile to Vorkuta. Until his departure for Germany, Johann had lived all of his working life there as a miner.

I was surprised to learn that Vanya, the German, yearned terribly for his life in Russia. Every day he told us of the friends he had left behind in the tundra. In Germany, as a person who had suffered under the Soviet regime, Vanya was given a one-room apartment, rent-free. He had bought himself a car and furniture and lived well. In Russia he could only have dreamed of all that. How could a man, in prosperous Westphalia, yearn for Vorkuta, a place gripped by frost and surrounded by barbed wire?

In his cozy and comfortable apartment the Soviet German would knock back a full glass of vodka, take a bite of a sour pickle and complain to us, "There's no one to talk to here. Everybody's busy, thinking only about what they can earn. What about the mind? No, I can't go on like this. We had it better in Vorkuta."

Vanya was particularly fond of recalling the events that occurred each year on May 9 — the national holiday when Soviets celebrate their victory over Nazi Germany. In the miners' hostel where Vanya lived a collection was always taken up on the morning of the holiday — everyone contributing fifty rubles for vodka and snacks.

"How much shall we take from Vanya?" someone would ask.

"Nothing," people replied, "he's a German. For him, this is a day of mourning. Let him drink on us."

Toward the end of April, Alex warned me that the next day I should be ready for a serious ordeal.

"I advise you to have a good night's sleep," he said, "and do not drink any spirits."

I immediately recalled Sergei's instruction about having to submit to the lie detector test. So my turn had come!

Fortunately, I had a bad toothache at the time and so the next morning I swallowed a couple of tablets of painkillers and cheerfully washed them down with a glass of vodka. I had a sure excuse. My cheek was visibly swollen from the infection, and it is a well-known fact that vodka is the best painkiller. If anything should happen I could always plead that I just couldn't stand the pain.

Alex drove me to a special villa that belonged to military intelligence and handed me over to a couple of Americans. One of them them had an artificial leg and wore a ring with a beautiful ruby—a sign that he belonged to the special troops of the United States Army. The other wore glasses and a white smock and looked like a medical doctor. I was taken into a room that had one wall that was a mirror. They sat me in an armchair at a table and attached wires to my chest, wrists, and forehead. The wires led to an apparatus about the size of a briefcase which had been placed on the table. The one-legged man then disappeared—I surmised that he was watching me from the other side of the mirrored wall. His colleague asked me some preliminary questions, then stood behind me and warned: "You are now going to undergo a small test. There is nothing to worry about since it will not do you any harm. I will ask questions and you must—quickly and without thinking—reply with a simple 'yes' or 'no.' Do you understand? Just 'yes' or 'no.' Answer immediately, without a second thought. Please sit quite still, without moving."

The apparatus on the table was turned on and a tape began to roll out of it. I glanced at myself in the mirror. My face didn't show the slightest trace of fright. I was bearing up well.

"You are Tumanov, Oleg Alexandrovich?"

"Yes."

"You were born November 12, 1944?"

"Yes."

"You completed courses in the KGB in 1964?"

"No."

"You were a member of the Communist Party?"

"No."

"Your uncle works for the KGB?"

"Yes."

"Are you a homosexual?"

"No."

"Are you deceiving us?"

"No."

"Malofeyev is a relative of yours?"

"Yes."

"He drew you into collaboration with the KGB?"

"No."

"You ran away from your ship because you like to live in the West?"

"Yes."

"You love your native land?"

"Yes."

"You agreed to carry out tasks for the KGB because you love your country?"

"No."

"Do you consider yourself an honest man?"

"Yes."

"The girl you used to date in Moscow before you were called into the army is called Tatyana?"

"Yes."

"Your parents knew nothing about your intention to go to the West?"

"Yes."

"Are you forced to lie sometimes?"

"Yes."

I sat there as if I were in the electric chair. My hands rested on the arms of the chair. The leads were attached to my body and the recorder was writing out my sentence. Or my acquittal? It was very easy to fail. One or two mistakes and that would be the end. They would begin to suspect me and start digging into my past. I would lose their trust in me, and that would be the end of a former sailor's career as a spy. The lie detector had helped to "break" better people than Tumanov. In 1964 the clever instrument had for a long time ruined the life of a defector from the KGB, Yuri Nosenko, who had offered his services to the Americans.

A member of the American department of the Second Chief Director-ate of the KGB (counterintelligence), Nosenko was on an official assignment in Geneva when he sent United States intelligence a previously agreed-upon coded telegram. A few days later, he secretly moved from Switzerland to West Germany where he was put up in one of the special apartments in Frankfurt (possibly the same one as I had). Nosenko was soon put through a lie detector test. By then he had been collaborating with the CIA for almost two years and had performed some priceless services for the Americans. It was, however, Nosenko's misfortune that another KGB man, by the name of Golitsyn, had already come over to the Americans and had told them that the next defector from Moscow would be a "plant"—an agent sent by the Lubyanka. Whether Golitsyn had any basis for his assertion, or had simply invented the story to raise his price, is still not known. But Nosenko's fate has become a classical example of the extreme suspicion of American intelligence services and their fears of possible penetration by Soviet agents.

Suspecting nothing, Nosenko was his own worst enemy. He was convinced of his importance to the CIA and reckoned that his screening was a mere formality. Thus, he treated both the lie detector and the routine questioning very casually, and his replies to simple questions aroused suspicion. For example, on one occasion he described himself as a lieutenant-colonel, but at other times said he was a captain. Although Nosenko had worked in Moscow against the Americans, he didn't know which floors of the United States embassy were occupied by the *rezidentura* (the special services) and was not able to describe the canteen in the main KGB building in Dzerzhinsky Square. The counterintelligence officers of the CIA were so concerned that they kept Nosenko under investigation for nearly five years, leaving him in solitary confinement for many months. The CIA was convinced that he had been sent from Moscow, first, to divert suspicion from Lee Harvey Oswald (who was at the time suspected of being connected with the KGB), and second, to protect the Lubyanka's mole, who had penetrated deep into the innermost part of the American intelligence service.

It was not until the third time that Nosenko was subjected to the lie detector test that his torturers were satisfied. Only then, in August 1968, did the results turn out to be positive. Although external counterintelligence continued to regard Nosenko as a "disinformer," he was transferred to a free way of life. It was not until much later that counterintelligence ceased keeping Nosenko under observation.

At that time I had no idea of the suffering endured by traitors. But I came very close to being in Nosenko's position.

Sometimes the same questions were repeated. Sometimes it seemed that the questions had already been asked, but no, two or three words had been changed and the sense of the question was completely reversed. But you can't stop to think, the pace has to be kept at Olympic levels. I tried little tricks to gain time. Instead of answering "yes" or "no" I would make a longer reply. My tricks didn't work: My replies were immediately cut off.

"You served on the destroyer *Spravedlivy*?"

"Yes."

"Your father's name is Alexander Vasilevich?"

"Yes."

"In Moscow you had meetings with your KGB controller in a safe apartment?"

"No."

"You prefer blondes?"

"No."

"Do the palms of your hands often sweat?"

"No."

"As a child were you expelled from school for bad behavior?"

"Yes."

"Are you afraid of spiders?"

"No."

"Do KGB officers seem to you to be important people?"

"Yes."

"In your sex life do you avoid doing things regarded as perversions?"

"Yes."

"If you are lying are you ready to accept severe punishment?"

"Yes."

This torture continued for about an hour. Finally the man in the horned-rimmed glasses came out from behind me, switched off the apparatus, and detached me from the wires. Almost simultaneously, Alex and the one-legged man with the ring reappeared. Ignoring me, the three of them began to study the tape. I thought there was something wrong because their faces had the same kind of strained expressions I imagined surgeons might have when they had finished an operation, but were not yet sure if the patient was going to live.

Then Alex rolled up the tape and slipped it into his pocket. "Let's go and eat," he snapped. In the car I naïvely asked what the trouble was.

"This is an extremely important stage in you screening," he replied without the suspicion of a smile. "In principle, it is impossible to deceive this system. It's very perceptive, and it looks as though it is not quite satisfied with you. There are some questions that have arisen, and we," he sighed, "will have to go on to the second round. It means a lot of work."

In a couple of days we began again from the beginning. Sam, the "bigwig," turned up again and after him Boris, the "airman." Alex, in the maniacal manner of the mentally ill, started filling out my personal history forms again, extracting details of my background. If some of the trifling details didn't match what I had previously told Alex he would call a halt and attempt to catch me in a deliberate lie. I was convinced that they were groping in the dark. I had not, thus far, given them even the slightest grounds for suspicion.

I realized that my screening had come to a successful conclusion when, on a pleasant spring day in 1966, Alex announced: "You are invited to visit the 'Svoboda' radio station in Munich."

In those days, Svoboda was still a branch of the American intelligence services and under their complete control. Thus, a person of dubious character would never have been allowed to visit. The invitation had to be regarded as a clear gesture of confidence.

I arrived in Munich, accompanied by George Perry, and settled into a modest guest house on the Leopoldstrasse. The radio station was then situated in a building at the old airport on the Lilienthalstrasse. At the station, I was led through crowded, smokey rooms, and introduced as if I were a person of some importance. "This is Oleg Tumanov. He has just arrived from the Soviet Union." In those days a person from the USSR was eyed with wonderment. Russian tourists and official travellers shied away from Svoboda's correspondents like the plague. Because there were practically no new émigrés, everyone wanted to see a live listener from Russia and to talk to a fellow countryman.

On one occasion during supper, my future immediate boss, Alexander Bakhrak, asked me: "What do you think of the problem of anti-Semitism in the Soviet Union?"

I was at a loss as to how to answer such questions. I had not had enough experience in life and my range of interest was rather narrow. What had I seen apart from school, a design bureau, and service in the navy? There was certainly no anti-Semitism at school. I recalled that the Jewish boys I knew were not treated any differently from the others. In the design bureau I had also noticed nothing of the kind. And in the navy I had never come across a single Jew. Perhaps they were called up into a different service?

"There is no anti-Semitism in Russia," I assured Bakhrak heatedly. He must have thought me very naïve or very dishonest.

On the whole, however, the people at Svoboda seemed to have been satisfied with me. I soon received an official invitation to work at the radio station, which I regarded as an incredible success. But before that some other changes took place that are worth recounting.

Volodya Krysanov at last received an appointment at the American consulate and had begun to look forward to an imminent departure to the United States—the land of unlimited possibilities where he would immediately open his own business. He was in high spirits when he went with Alex to apply for a visa. To pass the time Volodya was fond of telling stories about Jews—funny anecdotes which all had a similar moral: Jews were good for nothing.

On this great day, he wanted to share his happiness with everyone around him. But there was something he couldn't understand: why did Alex keep treading on his foot, and why did the consul's face seem strangely frozen and flushed? He decided that it meant that the men were enjoying his anecdotes.

What Volodya did not know was that the consul was a Jew, and a Zionist at that, and that the Siberian's anecdotes were nearly giving him an apoplectic fit. Krysanov's documents were naturally shelved. He wasn't going to see California anytime in the near future. After the experience, my furious (but not in the least abashed) friend declared that he would never set foot in the United States—he would go to Sweden instead. Incidentally, in Sweden, Volodya achieved his dream—he started a business and became a millionaire.

After seeing Volodya off to Stockholm, the "Russian German" Vanya Weimer and I left the airport and went to my apartment. There we drank to our friend's health and wished him well in his new life. Suddenly, Vanya became sad and begged me to let him telephone Vorkuta.

"Is that really possible?" I asked, forgetting that we were in an apartment that belonged to the American intelligence services.

"We can try," Vanya insisted. "Just dial the number of the telephone exchange . . . that's it . . . now ask for the Soviet Union and then the town of Vorkuta."

Incredible as it may seem, a few hours later, Vanya—tears running down his face—was actually talking to the woman in charge of the miners' hostel where he had lived. I remember this incident because one month later Alex called me from Munich, where I was soon to live, to inform me that I was to go to Frankfurt for a second lie detector test. He was furious: "To phone to Russia from a safe house belonging to the American intelligence! No, I can't recall anything like that." Fortunately, once he was satisfied that it had simply been a drunken escapade, and that I had not spoken on the phone, I was left in peace with no unpleasant consequences.

At the beginning of May 1966, Alex handed me an official notice from Radio Svoboda, signed by the head of the administration department, Jean Lecache. It said that I was invited to go to work for them and that eventually, if I proved to be satisfactory, they were willing to conclude a permanent contract with me. In the meantime, they offered me a probationary position.

"You are in luck, young man," Alex commented. "There aren't many twenty-two-year-old émigrés who have received such an offer. This is not a factory or an NTS printshop. It is a very prestigious, well-paid job. What do you think of it?"

"I'm very happy!" My eyes were really glistening. Success, as in the past, had carried me away.

"Then get your things together and sign this paper."

Alex handed me a paper which contained an agreement not to reveal anything of what had happened to me from December to May—the time when I was in the hands of the Americans. It further stated that if I breached the agreement, I could be sent to prison or fined twenty-five thousand Marks.

The next day he handed me the blue passport of a political émigré, a document that afforded me far more rights than the previous yellow passport of a refugee I had been carrying. Things could not have been going better.

A "Free" Man

When I joined Svoboda (Radio Liberty), employees were divided into three categories: Negroes, mulattos, and whites. Strange as it may seem, these categories had nothing to do with race or skin color. Negroes were hired under contracts according to German law. They were not provided with free housing, were obligated to pay their own taxes, and had to arrange for their own insurance. Mulattos were more privileged. As a rule, they had been hired in England, France, Spain, or another country, and were provided with free, furnished accommodations. Half of their insurance was paid for and they also enjoyed other benefits. Whites were in the best position. Mainly Americans, these employees received contracts based on United States standards, lived in beautiful apartments or villas, and drove luxurious cars—all, of course, for free.

In 1966, provision was made in the Radio Liberty budget for special funds to be used for renewing staff through the introduction of young people from behind the "iron curtain"—refugees, émigrés, and people who had refused to return to Russia. I was the first employee to be hired through the renewal program.

Willi Klump, an American of German origin, was in charge of this campaign. Radio Liberty had provided "white" Willi with a large apartment on the aristocratic Koenigenstrasse. On the floor below his apartment was an extra-small room for a servant. Willi invited me to stay with him at the outset, thus his servant-apartment became my first home in Munich. A bed, a cupboard, a little table, and a chair—that was all there was room for in the tiny space.

At the beginning of my employment I was assigned to Max Rallis, the head of the department for audience research. In 1971, Rallis and his team were transferred to Paris, but when I first arrived, they occupied a detached three-story mansion, discretely guarded by hefty looking young marines, on the Leopoldstrasse. Rallis's department sought listeners from around the world and questioned them about the effectiveness of the programs. The department was always headed by a man from the CIA, and department researchers had their own secret budget — all of this I learned much later.

I was allotted a room, brought a pile of papers with the transcripts of broadcasts and some tapes, and asked to analyze the materials according to a set plan. I was to give my opinion, both in terms of content and how the text was read. For instance, was the intonation correct? They asked me to study the output of Radio Liberty "in a fresh, straightforward way," and to suggest ways to improve the broadcasts to the USSR. One of my suggestions, which was to include regular programs for young people in the broadcasts, appealed to them immediately, and I was later entrusted with responsibility for producing those programs.

In the beginning I was supervised by one of Rallis's deputies, an Englishman named David. He would bring me the material, and in good Russian, with hardly an accent, give me all sorts of useful advice. One day, however, David disappeared without a trace. At the time I still did not fully understand what was going on around me — that I could not count on people speaking frankly or on their even slightly trusting me. The fashionably dressed and well-groomed Americans who worked in the department would at best greet me with a casual "hello." And I didn't always get that. For that reason, I did not immediately understand why the disappearance of David had caused such a fuss. Only some months later, when I was regarded as one of them, was it whispered to me that David had apparently been working for Soviet intelligence and had for some reason been urgently recalled to Moscow.

That was the first, but by no means the last, occasion when someone would suddenly disappear from Radio Liberty or Radio Free Europe, later to "surface" in some socialist country as an agent of the special services. One day it might be a Pole, the next a Czech, a Bulgar, a Lithuanian, or a Russian.

Twenty years later I too would unexpectedly disappear from Munich. Who would be next?

In those days, Radio Liberty and Radio Free Europe were the center of attention for the intelligence services of the countries of the Communist bloc. In the West, these radio stations were regarded as the principal "weapons of mass persuasion" in the never-ending ideological war. Moscow had its own shock-troops — including foreign broadcasts in dozens of languages, publishing houses, newspapers, and magazines that spread Communist ideas around the world. Brought up to the front line, Radio Liberty and Radio Free Europe were called on both to counter the "red propaganda" and to strike "preemptive blows," inform-ing listeners objectively about the situation in the "socialist camp." It would be no exaggeration to say that members of the Soviet Politburo feared "Liberty" more than any other American weapon.

When I had completed my month's trial with Max Rallis, I went to take my leave. Grey-haired and overweight, Max strutted around his office, smoke emanating from his pipe, conveying an attitude of self-confidence and strength that could only come from an American who knew his own worth. He thanked me for my work in measured terms and told me that I would now be at the disposal of the programming department of Radio Liberty.

"But you know," he stopped in front of my chair, "I would advise you to choose a different road. Go and study. We will help you get a stipend. There's a good university in Munich and a quite respectable hostel for students. You have a good command of languages. Believe me, that would be of much more use in your future than working in the snakepit that you are being offered."

"Snakepit?"

"Yes, Mr. Tumanov, precisely that. I know what I'm talking about. You are going to find it very difficult there, and you will often recall my words."

What could I say to Mr. Rallis? Obviously he really wished me well. The American secret agent who gave such advice to a young Russian émigré was acting against the interests of his "office," but spies are also human, so why should they not occasionally display a certain weakness? By calling the radio station (actually a branch of the special services) a collection of poisonous snakes Rallis seemed to be breaking the "rules of the game." His frank talk simply stunned me. But, alas, I could not take advantage of his advice. It was a tempting thought—to become a student, acquire a profession, learn some languages, make a career for myself . . . but my task did not provide for that. It required me to go and live in the "snakepit."

"Thank you, Mr. Rallis. But it will be better for me if I go and work for a time among my fellow countrymen. Maybe it will turn out alright."

"You just don't know them," the American shook his head reproachfully. "It's one thing to drink vodka with them and quite another to work on the same team. They will chew you up, spit you out, and trample you into the ground."

"All the same, I think I'll try it. After all, it will never be too late to take advantage of your advice."

The next morning Willi Klump drove me to the Lilienthalstrasse. After I had filled out a form in the personnel department the time came for me to meet my new immediate bosses. The news department of the

Russian service was then headed by a veteran of Radio Liberty, Alexander Bakhrak, who had once worked in Paris as a literary secretary to the great Ivan Bunin. His deputy was the young Alexander Peruansky. They worked in the same room, where Bakhrak, concealed by a copy of *Le Figaro*, was practically always dozing off, while Peruansky gave the appearance of furious activity.

When I timidly entered their room, Bakhrak only glanced around his *Figaro*. "Sasha, take care of the young man."

Peruansky was happy to deal with me. He understood at once that he was facing a young man who was capable of doing absolutely nothing. Such a person could have his nose rubbed in the dirt a thousand times a day, underlining his inability to carry out the simplest instructions.

"Oh, you don't speak German? That's a great pity, because you won't be able to write commentaries. What about translating agency reports from the English? Also not. What a pity! What can you do then? Who sent you? Oh, the Americans!"

This latter piece of information slightly reduced his arrogance. Everyone was afraid of the Americans, tried to ingratiate themselves with them, and didn't go against them. All the same, Peruansky was disappointed. He had already gotten what pleasure he could out of my helplessness and now he couldn't imagine what to do next to this mere boy whom "the Americans had sent." At last he found a way out.

"Try to write something about your impressions of Soviet life. Whatever you like. Just a couple of pages. I'll give you three days. You can write here or at home. It's all the same."

It seemed that Peruansky had already made up his mind that I was useless. His skepticism increased when three days later I handed him the painfully produced text of my first commentary. He skipped through it, threw it in the wastepaper basket, and with an air of disgust, delivered this sentence:

"No, that's not of interest to anybody. We don't write like that."

But the time to get rid of me had not yet come, so Peruansky delivered the young probationer into the care of one of his colleagues.

"Prince Volkonsky will take care of you," he said offhandedly.

Well! It was only in books that I had read about people with such titles. Prince Volkonsky. He must be a descendant of the hero of Leo Tolstoy's *War and Peace*. And he had been instructed to help me? My imagination vividly sketched the picture. Into the room would come a handsome, stately man in a morning coat, patent-leather shoes, a perfect part in his hair, and a diamond ring on his finger. He would be followed by a suite of servants and secretaries.

"*Bonjour, M'sieu,*" the prince would address me in French.

And what should I reply? "Good day, your Majesty"?

The door to my allotted room opened and a man I did not know, about twenty-eight years of age, shyly squeezed through. He was wearing washed jeans, an old faded T-shirt, and well-worn shoes. His unkempt dark hair did not give the slightest hint of having been combed.

"Are you Tumanov?"

"Yes, that's me."

"They've sent me to give you some help. My name is Oleg Volkonsky." He offered me his hand and went on absent-mindedly, "I work here as a translator and I am very glad that I now have the opportunity to tell them all to go to hell."

The prince turned out to be a great fellow. He didn't conceal his pleasure that he had been told to spend the whole day with me, going around the radio station and acting as a guide, instead of sweating over translations. He had, in fact, descended from the princely line so famous in Russia. But in 1939, the year when Oleg came into the world, his émigré parents, who had no real roots, lost practically everything they had. Thus, the only reminder Oleg had of his brilliant ancestry was his high-sounding title. I remained on friendly terms with Volkonsky right up until he left Liberty in 1973.

Oleg was conscientious. He took me around the archive, the library, and the technical services, and introduced me to all his friends. Gradually I began to get my bearings, to know who was who, and made some friends. I developed especially good relations with two former officers of General Vlasov's army, Leonid Pylayev and Andrei Menchukov, and with Igor Glazenap, who had found himself in Germany after being a prisoner of the Nazis. Igor's ancestors, who were also well born, had come to Russia from Germany during the eighteenth century, in the time of the Empress Catherine II. Pushkin himself had mentioned them in his works. Pylayev was in this respect the complete opposite of Glazenap: He was, as they say, "without kith or kin." But he had a very colorful personality. He composed songs, played the guitar, was a virtuoso at swearing, and in general resembled a real tough character. He drove a black Opel that had had a side window replaced with a piece of plywood, and had also gained notoriety for having acted with Yul Brenner in the 1959 Hollywood film *The Road.* After having received twenty-five hundred Marks for his performance—a decent sum in those days— Leonid hired a cameraman and two tarts, and shot a pornographic film in which he played the principal role. He loved to show his production in the Radio Liberty garage, where he would set up a projector, tables with drinks and snacks, and invite all his friends. No half-measures for Leonid!

It was Pylayev who warned me that the practice of informing on people not only flourished at Radio Liberty, but was encouraged by the Americans as one of the more effective forms of counterintelligence.

"No matter where you are, never say anything good about the Soviet Union," Leonid urged me. "In any company there will inevitably be one person who will report your words to the security service." Pointing out an employee known as Cain, Leonid once said, "He will try to make friends with you, but keep your distance, he is the number one informer."

Apart from that I was warned that I should be alert, even at home, because the security people had keys to all apartments occupied by Radio Liberty employees, and prophylactic searches were carried out when the occupants were absent. Sometime later I learned the merit of this warning.

There was a certain element of luck in my finally being kept on at the radio station as a permanent employee. From the beginning it was obvious that I was of no value as a commentator. I knew no relevant foreign languages and none of the skills required for radio broadcasting. But someone suddenly noticed my voice and suggested trying me out as an announcer. Although I had little hope for success I sat down at the microphone. As miraculous as it might seem, my unplanned performance drew unanimous praise. My voice was exactly what was needed for talking to Soviet listeners. It was deep, even, and powerful, and most importantly, it could be heard clearly through the jamming.

Those who wished me well, it seemed, breathed a sigh of relief. Tumanov could be used as a Liberty announcer. So I chose a pseudonym, Valeri Shulgin, and began to broadcast, first with others' materials and gradually with my own commentaries.

In the autumn of 1966, Willi Klump informed me that they had found a detached house for me. It turned out to be a comfortable two-story villa with a garden in Munich's student quarter. For one hundred Marks a month I was now able to live in comfortable conditions. In the beginning the house was mine alone because they had not yet succeeded in recruiting any other new arrivals for Radio Liberty.

I moved the best furniture into the room I had chosen on the second floor. Next to it was a beautifully furnished drawing room with a fireplace and a bar. I had never dreamed of living in greater luxury. It was not until the beginning of the next year that two Americans were moved in to join me. They were taking a course at the Munich Institute for the Study of the Soviet Union. The director of the institute was the grandson of the famous "white" Admiral Kolchak. I began attending lectures on philology, economics, and politics. It was then that I discovered for myself a huge and previously unknown era of Russian literature in the works of Bulgakov, Zamyatin, Averchenko, Bunin, and Babel—all of which were banned in the Soviet Union.

One of my American roommates was the son of a rich surgeon from California. He spoke good Russian and was hoping for a career in the diplomatic service. The other, a Jew, wanted to buy a piece of land in some exotic corner of Colorado and open a restaurant.

We usually all came together for our evening meal, when each of us cooked for himself in accordance with his financial resources and taste. I generally had soup out of a packet and two or three sandwiches. The future restaurant owner was a vegetarian and would sadly consume a dish of oatmeal porridge. But the Californian always prepared a real feast—a nice piece of steak, a huge bowl of salad, ice cream. It was the first time I had come across such habits. In the USSR we had different customs. If we were sitting at one table we were obliged to offer each other what we had. In the West it was each man for himself.

At the beginning of 1967, I became a permanent employee of Radio Liberty. They concluded a lifelong contract with me and fixed my salary at eleven hundred Marks a month. Things could not have been going better.

My first girlfriend in Munich was the daughter of an important foreign ministry official from among the Sudeten Germans. Her name was Ursula, Ushi for short. She had chestnut hair, a good figure, pleasant ways, and was very sensual. I dated Ushi for two years and would have married her if it hadn't meant leaving the radio station. She and her parents insisted on that, and on my entering the university, which was of course impossible.

Toward winter's end, Willi Klump invited me to his office.

"This is how it is, Oleg," he began, "You were hired to work in Germany, which means you are on the 'black list' and are regarded as a 'negro.' Right?"

"Yes," I agreed cautiously, not understanding what he was getting at.

"So you don't have the right to free accommodation and other privileges. But we have exercised our brains and recalled that you arrived here from Libya, didn't you? That means that we can say that you were hired there in your contract. Agreed?"

"I wasn't hired in Libya . . . "

"Don't let that bother you. A pure formality. But you will at once be given a different status. Just sign this paper and you will receive a two-room apartment right away. Hurry up, Oleg."

A little later I had a housewarming in a very comfortable apartment on Terezienstrasse and moved up into the category of "mulattos." I obtained a loan of two thousand Marks from the bank to furnish it properly. Ursula enjoyed helping me. I lived about a year and a half in that apartment. Just before the Soviet invasion of Czechoslovakia I was offered accommodations in a new building on Elektrostrasse. It was a really super apartment—convenient, well lit, with modern furniture.

At about the same time Radio Liberty moved to a new building on Arabellastrasse. The building had been built originally as a hospital, but when the city could not afford it, the Americans took it over so that Radio Liberty and Radio Free Europe could be housed under the same roof. With the move, changes also took place in the staff of the news department. Bakhrak was sent off to head the Paris office: He was succeeded by Peruansky. These changes served only to heighten the hostility between our department (news and commentary for the first thirty minutes of each hour) and the so-called Russian editorial department (programs about culture, science, history, and sport for the second thirty minutes). Our rivals had an extremely high opinion of themselves but considered us to be second-class journalists, pitiful reporters.

The director of the Russian editorial, Witold Ryser, had had his eye on me and decided to entice me over to his department. For a start he suggested to Radio Liberty's top people that I be sent, in the company of an experienced correspondent, Alexander Mikhelson, to London, Paris, and Zurich to prepare a series of programs about the life of the average European.

"It is time to show Tumanov the world," Ryser explained. "He hasn't seen anything apart from Germany, after all." There could be no objection in the face of that logic. Peruansky, guessing his rival's clever plan, ground his teeth, but released me for the two-week trip.

My main task on that trip was to learn. I had to carry Mikhelson's heavy tape recorder around, help him with his interviews, and try to remember everything connected with the journalistic profession. I did all that. And I also had the great pleasure of seeing the sights of the English capital, breathing the irreplicable atmosphere of the boulevards of Paris, and admiring the mountain landscapes of Switzerland. It was a wonderful trip! And it was not even spoiled by the fact that after my return Peruansky begrudged my attachment to the Russian editorial department and considered me a traitor for a long time—although I did not yield to Ryser's persuasion and remained in the news department.

Opportunity Knocks

The 1968 Soviet invasion of Czechoslovakia marked the turning point in my career at Radio Liberty. Soviet tanks crushed the Czechs' and Slovaks' attempts to achieve freedom, but I rode on their armor into the ranks of the outstanding journalists at Liberty. Now there's a strange paradox!

At the time of the invasion I was carrying out the duties of an announcer, occasionally writing commentaries. In short, I was at the beck and call of more important colleagues. But my two years at the radio station had not gone to waste. I had watched experienced journalists at work, studied their material, and drawn some conclusions. Internally, I had reached the point of moving from the category of apprentice to that of professional. I needed only the occasion, a signal, and some stimulus.

Late on the night of August 20, 1968, the telephone rang in my apartment.

"Oleg, this is Peruansky speaking. Come immediately to the office."

"What's happened? War? A fire? Trouble?"

"For God's sake, skip the questions. You will find out when you get here."

Having decided, still half asleep, that the head of the news department wanted to make a fool of me, I cursed him roundly and was about to put the receiver down when I heard:

"Soviet troops have occupied Czechoslovakia. Their tanks are already on the streets of Prague. You understand how this may end up."

Peruansky had the bad habit of telephoning his subordinates at night—sometimes with good reason, sometimes without. He would be drinking somewhere and at the same time would dial someone.

"Are you out of your mind, Sasha? Have you had a drop too much?"

His reply, in coarse language and sober voice was simply, "Oleg, I beg you, come as quick as you can. I am phoning everyone, but I get no answers, and time is running out."

At that time the news department worked only one shift—the daytime one. At night they played the tapes with the old, and at best the evening information. This arrangement suited everybody because it allowed them to work without undue pressure. When I arrived at the office that night I found only a very worried Peruansky and a sleepy Alexander Neimirok, who just couldn't believe his chief's words about the tanks in Prague.

"What if it's just provocation?" he kept asking.

Peruansky was relying on information from worldwide new agencies but he was staggered by the very limited and contradictory reports. He had himself been dragged out of bed by such a high-ranking boss that he could hardly speak, only stutter and swear.

At last he made a decision: "We must immediately change the news list. Oleg, you rewrite the whole transmission. Neimirok, write the commentaries."

"But what if it is a provocation?" Neimirok wouldn't give up. "If I write the commentaries and it turns out to have been a lie or a bluff in the morning I will be in big trouble."

Those words summed up the principal aim of the majority of the people working for Liberty—to keep, at any price, as far as possible away from extreme situations. The information from Czechoslovakia was very scrappy and not well checked. The boss possibly had a hangover. Why get mixed up in it? You might lose your job.

I agreed at once to prepare a report of the events taking place in Czechoslovakia, which was a neighboring country, and to record all the news again on to a tape.

A little later Robert Tuck, director of the Russian service, arrived. He marched around the empty offices of the service, looked at the three of us, gave us no instructions, but looked extremely worried. We then received some fresh information from Radio Free Europe. The information had arrived through their channels and included sounds of shooting, the shouts of the crowd, and tank motors. West German television started to transmit special programs. No doubt now remained: The Soviet Army had invaded the territory of a neighboring sovereign state.

Toward morning, details began to come in. It appeared that, along with the Soviet troops, troops from other countries in the Warsaw Pact were also taking part in the acts of intimidation. Alexander Dubçek had been arrested. The Czechoslovak government had been transferred to Moscow. The few centers of resistance were being crushed mercilessly. Every hour I recorded fresh sensational reports on tape, and the tape went straight on the air. At ten o'clock in the morning I handed off to colleagues who now appeared in the office. We went off to have a brief rest, returning to our places at lunchtime.

Now it became much easier to work. The news came in a stream of statements and eyewitness reports. Peruansky handed me a bundle of agency reports, saying, "Quickly, quickly. Translate them into Russian and get them ready for broadcast."

"But maybe it would be better to prepare the regular 'Meetings with our listeners,'" I suggested cautiously to him, "to have a heart-to-heart talk . . . "

I deliberately stirred things up. In those days it was still difficult for me to translate quickly from the English. Heart-to-heart talks were simpler.

"That's it, we'll do that!" Peruansky was unexpectedly pleased. "That will be a reflection of our own position."

In my commentary I wrote that the Kremlin had made a tragic mistake that would do it great harm, that good sense would triumph in the end, and that the sympathies of the whole world were now on the side of the Czechs and Slovaks. I didn't have to force myself or write something that contradicted my own opinions—I wrote what I believed. The strategy of intimidating neighboring states, first tried in Hungary and now being applied in Czechoslovakia, would later meet with failure in Afghanistan. Afghanistan began in Budapest and Prague.

My commentary was broadcast. Late that evening we were called together by Robert Tuck, director of the Russian service. He announced that he had been instructed to put all our efforts into reporting events in Czechoslovakia. We would be working in two twelve-hour shifts— midnight to eight o'clock in the morning and eight o'clock to midnight.

"In addition," and here Tuck's voice took on a triumphant note, "we have instructions to make use of the full power of Liberty's transmitters. America will spend whatever is needed to ensure that any jamming of our programs is suppressed."

This time (unlike the Cuban crisis) the West did not receive an impertinent challenge from Moscow and didn't attempt to respond to force with force. Nonetheless, certain precautionary maneuvers were taken. But they relied mainly on the propaganda war. They had to demonstrate to the whole world, primarily the Soviet population, the Kremlin's treachery, the aggressive nature of communism, and the Soviet Union's expansionist foreign policy. These themes were already part of anti-Soviet propaganda, but now they did not seem like the usual rhetoric—they were being illustrated by the tanks in Prague. From that point of view the West had made the right choice: the concentrated propaganda campaign inflicted a powerful blow to the positions taken up by Communists throughout the world.

At eight o'clock in the evening (Moscow time), which is the very best time for broadcasting because the largest number of listeners gather at their receivers, we were given permission to do a live broadcast. Until then all transmissions had been prerecorded. But now we had an unexpected problem: Our announcers flatly refused to broadcast "live."

There was a powerful psychological barrier. It was one thing to know that you were dictating text onto a tape—you could correct any mistakes—but it was quite different to communicate directly with the listeners. The responsibility was many times greater. Bob Tuck then recalled how we had worked on the night of the emergency and in particular my heroic efforts.

"Alright," he said to the veteran announcers. "You just put in some training and while you are doing it you will be replaced by this young man. Do you agree, Mr. Tumanov?"

That was my big chance and I couldn't let it get away.

The first program went on the air on August 23. On the other side of the glass separating the studio from the producer's control panel I could see the whole management of Radio Liberty, including the then president of the station, Walter Scott. They were drinking whiskey. People were visibly nervous. I was too. For the first time in the history of Liberty the announcer was speaking "live" to listeners. When I successfully completed the program there was no end to their delight.

"Magnificent, Oleg!"

Although it was already night the American bosses hauled us off to celebrate in one of the more expensive bars. From then on, for many days in a row, at exactly eight o'clock I took my place at the microphone.

"This is a special transmission devoted to the events in Czechoslovakia. From the studio of Radio Liberty, Oleg Tumanov. Here is the latest news." (I had by then dropped the "Valeri Shulgin" pseudonym.)

I now recall those events of long ago rather detachedly and unemotionally, but in fact the Soviet-Czechoslovak conflict might have grown into a major war. I remember very well that the American troops quartered in Bavaria were brought to a state of full battle readiness. A rumor went around Munich to the effect that the Russian tanks wouldn't stop at Prague but would advance further to the West. It would take them two hours to reach Munich. There was panic in the radio station and some especially impressionable people vanished from the city that day. Some left on the excuse of "illness"—others thought up other reasons. The older émigrés remembered very well what Stalin had done with the likes of them when they were found in Germany.

An employee of the London bureau of Radio Liberty, Leonid Finkelstein, who had recently been in Munich on business, phoned us from Great Britain suggesting: "Do as you like, friends, but it's more peaceful this side of the Channel."

It then turned out that the radio station did not have a single brave reporter capable of transmitting information from where the events were taking place. When management needed to send a correspondent to the border of Czechoslovakia, which thousands of refugees were crossing, they could not find a single candidate for the job. Everyone offered the job found a plausible excuse for refusing. In the end, to everyone's relief, a character by the name of Andrei Menchukov volunteered for the duty. He was a sports commentator, a freelancer, who was renowned because he won a bottle of vodka every day at chess. Actually not just for that. Menchukov had written a good book about the famous Soviet soccer goalkeeper, Lev Yashin, and published it at his own expense. He demanded only one concession from Liberty management—to be paid one hundred Marks for each report he sent in. They were actually prepared to pay him much more.

An announcement on Radio Liberty asked people to take in refugees from Czechoslovakia for a certain period. I took in a young man of about seventeen by the name of Karel. He lived with me for a couple of weeks and then went back home to Czechoslovakia.

Gradually the heat of events subsided. In Czechoslovakia, occupation authorities ruled the situation and a rigid censorship was introduced. Information had literally to be invented. Crowds of journalists hung around Radio Liberty and Radio Free Europe in the hope of learning something new. Their special attention was directed, of course, to people working in the Czech and Slovak departments of Radio Free Europe, but others were also in demand. For example, I was invited to give an interview on Danish television and a television magazine in that country published a picture of me on its cover.

Some time later it became clear that our titanic efforts to increase the power of our broadcasting transmitters and our "live" broadcasts had not worked because the Soviet jammers also brought in all their reserves and greatly increased their power to interfere. The total effect was nil. With that, my "live" broadcasts came to an end.

The enthusiasm created by the first live broadcast from Liberty was not, however, forgotten by station management. They increased my salary and later sent me to Great Britain for three months to improve my English and acquire a deeper knowledge of the Western way of life—at the station's expense, of course.

By the end of 1968, after having obtained agreement from the security service and Alex (I had phoned him), I wrote my first letter to my parents. I told them I was working for an American firm, that everything was fine with me, that there was no need to worry, and that henceforth we could exchange letters regularly. I was well aware that my letter would be first read by the KGB and that only later it might reach my parents.

At the beginning of the following year I received a reply from my father, written in an emphatically restrained manner. It seemed that the old chap seriously considered me a traitor or had received the corresponding instructions from the Lubyanka. My reply to his letter is preserved in the family archives. It was sent from Munich to Moscow on March 12, 1969. The letter read:

"Greetings, dear folks! I've just received your first letter and I am glad that we have established some kind of contact. I am glad that you are all, if not in the best of health, at least alive. And health is, as they say, a matter of time.

"I was rather surprised by your words, father—'when you turn yourself in and admit your guilt.' What guilt? What am I guilty of? Surely you don't think that I acted without thinking or took such an important step with my eyes closed? Certainly not! At that moment I thought of everything and of you too, knowing that we might never meet again and that I would not be able to support you in your old age. I knew, but I went ahead just the same so that it is irrevocable.

"I have always dreamed about the great world. About countries and peoples, encounters and travel—about many things my country couldn't give me. So I had to arrange it myself. And look at the results: In three years, I have been half way around Europe, I've been to Africa, England, and the United States of America. I have realized another of my dreams. I am now a journalist working for the radio, television, and the cinema. In Sweden they are now shooting a film based on my story. My reports are being read and listened to by thousands, if not millions, of people. For all that was it not worthwhile taking that step? Which of my friends can boast of such things? Which of them has seen so much? Which one will ever see it? Not one!

"Do you remember saying to me, 'Study, otherwise you will go on working for a miserable hundred rubles . . . ' So I am studying. I can speak three languages. I have a job and receive not that 'miserable hundred,' but roughly two thousand rubles a month. My brother, who has studied and worked for nearly twenty years, still can't buy himself a car and had to wait several years to have a two-room apartment for a family of three. I buy a new model each year and now have an American sports car and a three-room apartment just for myself.

"Next Sunday I am going away for ten days of skiing. By the way, I could choose between the mountain resorts of Switzerland and France. My friends in the Soviet Union can at best choose between the Carpathians and the Caucasus. Do you get the difference?

"I don't intend to lavish praise on the West: There are plenty of bad things here, but I have found what I sought. So let's leave that subject 'until you return.' I will return when I am sure that I can return at any time to the West, and when I am guaranteed the same freedom as I have here. That's it!

"Papa, I can't make head or tail of your illnesses. I phoned my doctor, but he's on holiday. As soon as I get back from Austria (on March 27) I'll call him again and ask his advice. Perhaps they have some new medications and new ways of treating people. Then I will write to you and try to send a parcel of medicines.

"Incidentally, you must send me your measurements. There are a mass of things here that you should have. I think that's all. I am hoping for a quick reply. And I expect letters from Igor, Volodka, Tanya, Tolka, and Seya. So tell them that.

"I embrace you and kiss you. Oleg."

I am now ashamed when I read that letter. It is false through and through, pompous and stupid. There was only one true statement in it: I really had always dreamed of travelling and in that sense one could say that my dream had been realized. In the letter I lied about going to the United States, about working for the cinema and television, about new models of cars that I changed each year. At the time I had a second-hand Ford Mustang, bought on the cheap.

Why did I have to lie? The fact was that the letter was written primarily for the benefit of American and German counterintelligence and secondarily for my parents. I felt disgusted with myself as I composed that rubbish. But what could I do — even in relations with people close to him a spy has to exercise cunning and be governed primarily by the interests of the business. Such is the nature of the devilish trade.

Actually, my parents occasionally wrote me letters, also dictated by the KGB. My father was invited to their office and asked to sign something. He obediently agreed. It was all part of the business of concealment.

The fact that I began to receive replies to my letters meant that Soviet intelligence had intercepted my signals, remembered me, and that the time would come when I would be summoned into activity. I had the feeling I would not have to wait long.

I was not mistaken.

Part II

Respected at Radio Liberty

Back to School in Karlshorst

January 1970. East Berlin. Karlshorst. We had not left the house for three days. We were really working—my KGB instructors and I. I was given three days to absorb a huge quantity of information, to receive and understand my tasks for the immediate future and the longer term, and to master the various channels of communication. And everything had to be committed to memory—without benefit of summaries or notes.

Under normal conditions it would have taken me at least two weeks to memorize so many names, addresses, special terms, and dates. But these conditions were not normal. There were just three days for the course of instruction and another four for practical lessons. I doubt whether any spy has ever been trained at such speed.

Each morning I had only enough time to quickly eat a light breakfast and drink a strong cup of coffee before Sergei was at my door, rosy-cheeked, and full of life and optimism.

"Greetings to the ideological enemy," was his noisy salutation. "So, are you ready for battle?"

"I'm ready," I would reply without any special enthusiasm.

Any business done in a rush was not particularly to my taste. I get tired of seeing a stream of documents and of taking in fresh information before grasping what had gone before. But there was no way out. I had to work.

We would sit facing each other at a table. He would open a briefcase and pull out documents and photographs. It seemed as though he had a dossier on every employee of Radio Liberty worthy of attention. He showed me photographs of my bosses, then provided exhaustive descriptions of each and advice about how to behave with them. He warned of the dangers some represented and indicated which ones I should get on friendly terms with.

"That's Peruansky, your immediate superior. Try to be on good terms with him, but keep your distance. He plays the part of being 'one of us,' but is, in fact, a double-dealer who is as treacherous as many Asians. If he needs to, he will snatch your seat from under you without a second thought. He will betray everything and everyone for the sake of his career. Peruansky was born in Teheran into a family of émigrés—a Russian doctor and an Iranian woman—and has had never lived in Russia. He was a member of the NTS but left the organization to make a career at Liberty. He has taken part in a number of campaigns against our country.

"Beware of Oleg Krasovsky. He is also a former member of the NTS and according to our information has been an active adviser to American counterintelligence in Southeast Asia. Before they came to Liberty, Victor and Tatyana Verbitsky worked for American military intelligence. It is quite possible that both have maintained those contacts.

"Bear in mind that your apartment may be 'bugged' periodically. You must, therefore, watch what you say. Study people carefully, paying particular attention to those who force themselves on you as friends. Be forthcoming with them, but take care."

As my first task, Sergei asked me to find out more about department "X," the monitoring service that recorded radio telephone conversations between Soviet military units in Germany and Eastern Europe. For a start I was to collect as full a dossier as possible on the people working in the department: their addresses, habits, weaknesses, faults, the registration numbers of their cars, and so forth. Then I was to try and penetrate deeper.

"But I beg you, Oleg," my instructor pleaded, "don't lose your head. Don't seem excessively curious. Don't make yourself a nuisance. Don't give rise to the slightest suspicion. Everything should come about naturally, as if of its own accord. The ideal way is to have a good friend there that you don't have to drag things out of. He will tell you all you need to know without noticing he's done it. Remember, counterintelligence conceals its objectives very thoroughly. If you come within the scope of its attention it can cost you dearly. Our trade requires patience above all else.

"You and I have unlimited time," Sergei continued. "There is no need to hurry. What you don't learn today you will learn tomorrow. We have a whole life ahead of us. Most important is that you maintain your position at the radio station for as long as possible. You should know that the Center values you highly."

We would take a short break for lunch and then start over again—names, descriptions, photos, advice, addresses. My head was spinning.

Much later, when I came to analyze these and other meetings I had in

Karlshorst I realized that, apart from purely professional training from my instructors, I was being brainwashed. Time after time they drummed into me the thought that the employees of Radio Liberty and Radio Free Europe were a gang of malicious, dangerous enemies of my country and that every employee deserved my contempt. The vast ideological apparatus that controlled everything even required that the KGB give an account of itself—its spy network and its agents. They were all controlled from the party headquarters in the Old Square.

Poor Sergei had to spend valuable time drumming one message into me over and over again: I was completely surrounded by scoundrels, traitors, and CIA hirelings. I believe that Sergei himself understood perfectly well that it would have been better to divide Radio Liberty employees into two groups—those who were really working for the special services and the rest. He understood this, but was afraid to disobey his instructions. And who wasn't in those days? And so we would mark time for hours in one place. He would read me the next "lesson" and I would obediently nod my head, letting his words float by while I glanced greedily at his briefcase, which contained what I really needed—precise, brief, concrete operational facts. A real spy's weapon.

Once we'd paid our dues to the ideological apparatus, we would permit ourselves a minute or so of relaxation. I would tell Sergei of my admiration for the émigrés of the "first wave," many of whom I had gotten to know well, for their genuine intellectual qualities, their high morals, and their genuine love for Russia, which was now lost to them forever. My colleague would sigh and scratch his head. He understood well how much our spiritually unfortunate country needed such people. But Sergei would always have the last word: "All the same Oleg, no matter how you look at it, they are all hirelings of American intelligence and have sold themselves for money."

Just try to prove whether or not they had sold themselves. Especially since the American intelligence services really did use Radio Liberty and Radio Free Europe as a branch of their organization—that axiom did not require proof.

It was easier for Sergei and me when we were discussing Nazi war criminals in Liberty or some of the "third wave" émigrés. Both really were capable of buying or selling anything. They had no moral principles, no intellectual baggage, and no feelings of patriotism. When we talked about such people we quickly found a common language. We could, if we had wished, catch any of them on our hook. But I was never required to do that. It was much more important for the Center to see who was attracted to those people and to whom they were drawn themselves. External counterintelligence did not have the right to let such people out of their sight, even for a moment.

In accordance with instructions from Moscow, Sergei, and all of my other operational leaders, diligently submitted me to the ideological treatment. Even without the various "treatments," I must admit that I never doubted the rightness of the cause I was serving.

On the fourth day at Karlshorst, Sergei introduced me to a new teacher. He was an elderly, reserved man who wore a dark gray suit that had obviously been purchased in a Soviet department store. Without beating around the bush he announced that he was going to teach me about what in the language of my new profession was known as "external observation." First he took a bundle of photographs out of his briefcase and laid them out before me. I let out a whistle in surprise. When had they been able to record my movements in Berlin on film, in such detail? There Sergei and I were leaving the building. There we were getting into the car. There we were going down the street, with the car's license plate and the name of the street clearly visible. There we were going into a bookstore. There I was standing near a counter with books, glancing through a brochure. There I was talking to Sergei. How could they have gotten that photograph? I clearly remember that there was no one else in the bookstore with us. What sort of a trick was this?

"You feel quite at home in Karlshorst," my new teacher explained calmly. "Your attention is slackened and you don't keep your eye on what's going on around you. It's not really your fault in this case, but it always is when it is a question of personal safety, and even more important when it concerns the safety of others connected with you. Actually, Sergei didn't do very well either: he only noticed the 'tail' once, through the shop window.

"Now we will go for a walk. You can go down any street in Karlshorst on one condition: make note of the places where you are able to notice me and my assistants. We will be close to you at all times, but at a certain distance. We will be playing the part of plainclothes detectives following you around."

Sergei and I wandered around the little township for a couple of hours as evening fell. Although I tried very hard, I only caught sight of my "tail" once. I thought that perhaps the "external observation" had lost us, but as soon as we returned home the new teacher appeared.

"Well, did you see me?"

"Not once," I said with a gesture of guilt.

"But I could draw a map of where you went. There were three of us following you. Did you catch sight of anyone?"

Hesitantly, I recalled a couple of characters who had struck me as being suspicious.

"No," he confirmed my incompetence decisively. "But don't worry about it. You will learn."

Hours of lectures about external observations and ways for defeating and getting around it followed. I am not going to repeat here the substance of those lectures because they have been described many times in other books on the subject, and I would guess that the methods used for defeating a "tail" are roughly the same for all intelligence services.

A few days later Sergei and I drove to the city in his car and spent time driving through the streets of Berlin. It was a sort of excursion. When we returned home he asked me if I had noticed that we were being followed. Again I blushed with shame: I had not thought that our excursion would also be an examination.

"Get used to it," the instructor advised me condescendingly. "You must check yourself regularly in the matter of being followed, and you must learn to do it to perfection."

The "professor of external observation" put me through some more practical exercises and taught me some tricks that involved quick changes of clothes and appearance. In the evenings we analyzed the day's "operations." I was praised only once: On the second day, the teacher's young men lost me in the town and I got back to the finish (the entrance to my house) without a "tail." He took this failure extremely painfully.

As a part of my external observation training I learned how to use camouflage clothing—jackets that are white on one side and dark brown on the other. You can change you appearance quickly with these jackets. I never had the occasion to use the jackets or even a beard or wig. I did, however, occasionally check my skills at evading shadows to keep my instincts sharp.

My instructor also suggested to me that one of the best places to safely meet "friends" to exchange information was in the forest, while hunting for mushrooms. I became an avid mushroom picker.

My next instructor turned out to be a chemist, and that was the name I gave him. He was a specialist in cyphers and secret writing. The "chemist" taught me how to use a cypher pad and other clever devices for special communications. One of his questions puzzled me.

"Have you by chance ever collected stamps?"

"No."

"That's a pity. I would advise you to take up such a hobby. It would provide you with an excuse for buying a good magnifying glass."

The Center had decided to use the ordinary postal service for urgent communications, and letters dispatched from Austria, Italy, and other countries had to have a special mark on them. If I found such a secret mark on an envelope I was instructed to steam the envelope open and look for a message in cypher—no bigger than the head of a match—hidden in one of the folds. The message could only be read with the aid of a powerful magnifying glass. They could have given me an "olive"—a special magnifying glass, a sort of miniature spy-glass—but the "olive" is a working instrument of special services and, therefore, is an undesirable piece of evidence. It would have been difficult for me to explain why I had such a device if I had been subjected to a sudden or secret search.

"So take up stamp collecting and buy yourself a magnifying glass," the "chemist" said. "It will be a combination of the pleasant and the useful."

Incidentally, that is what I did and never regretted it. In a few years I had a quite respectable collection of Russian and Soviet stamps, including some that were quite rare. For example, I succeeded in acquiring the first stamp issued in the last century. I became a passionate philatelist. And not just stamps. I started collecting examples of Russian paper money and securities, as well as Russian army badges, orders, and medals. Whenever I was in Paris, London, Copenhagen, or Vienna I would spend hours wandering through antique shops in search of objects of my passion. In fact this was sometimes useful in my main profession: the apparently unplanned stroll around shops selling antiques provided an opportunity to check my security before a meeting with people from the Center. I always remembered the advice I received in Karlshorst and was careful to make sure I was not being followed, especially if I was going to a meeting with messengers.

My training was coming to an end. Late one evening Sergei proposed that we go to a new Soviet film. We went in his car to the East Berlin office of Sovexportfilm, where at that time of night there were no employees except the night watchman who turned out to be both a projectionist and "our" man. We found ourselves in a tiny, comfortable cinema, in the center of which was a well-provided table with a bottle of brandy. We watched the film, eating and drinking at the same time. This scene was repeated during the course of my later visits to East Berlin—an excellent supper and, as desert, a new Soviet film. My instructors thus killed two birds with one stone. They helped to pass the time pleasantly and maintained my ideological level. It wasn't badly thought out.

I was offered the choice of flying from Copenhagen, Vienna, or Brussels, for my return to the West.

"They are tested routes," Sergei explained.

I chose Copenhagen because I had friends there, which could always serve to explain my presence in the Danish capital. I was handed an ordinary-looking ticket, except for the slightly distorted name on it. Instead of Tumanov, the name looked like Turnov or perhaps Temnov. I went to the airport at Schonefeld with Sergei, although the boys from the security group were surely circling around me. Sergei told me to put my passport away and in its place gave me some empty covers from a quite different passport. At border control, Sergei showed his official identity card. The border guard nodded and let him through. I then presented my false cover. With a serious expression, the border guard compared the nonexistent photograph with my face, stamped the empty cover with an exit visa and let me into the international area. The same performance took place when I checked my luggage.

Before taking off I drank a cup of coffee in the car with Sergei and gave him back the empty cover. We took leave of each other without fuss and I boarded the plane.

In Copenhagen I stayed in the Scandinavian airline's hotel for a day, using some of the time to buy a Nikon camera with a number of interchangeable lenses. I preferred the Nikon to the Minox and other miniature cameras purely out of concern for my safety. A Nikon does not arouse suspicion; it is simply evidence of its owner's respectable character and is better for photographing documents. I have never regretted my choice.

Lady Luck

In our business a great deal depends on chance, on luck. You can be a brilliantly trained and, in all respects, talented person but achieve absolutely nothing in the course a whole career. No results at all. Not a thing! And why? Simply because fortune has never smiled on you, the dice didn't roll your way, you didn't draw the lucky lot. The reverse is also true, however. More than one mediocre, undistinguished spy has made a brilliant career in the special services because the trump cards fell into his hands. Without making the slightest effort, he might, for instance, recruit the most valuable sources (ones that didn't turn out to be "moles"). While colleagues are continually being screened, exposed with a great fuss, sent into exile, or even put into prison, the lucky person, without making any special effort to observe the rules of conspiracy, may never come to the attention of counterintelligence. Awards and titles are showered on such people as if from the horn of plenty.

This is, of course, true to a greater extent in the case of officers in the legal *rezidenturas*—those who work under the cover of diplomatic and commercial missions, and within the offices of airlines and foreign firms. But good luck is essential to everyone to the same extent. The person who has it and can handle his good fortune with skill will enjoy great success.

As I have already said, luck has played no small role in my life. One day, as my first year at Radio Liberty was coming to an end, for instance, I was walking out of the library down a flight of stairs. To my surprise I saw a wallet lying on one of the steps. Others might have passed it, but I was the first to notice it. Rules at the station specified that anyone finding such a thing was to hand it over to the security service, but curiosity got the better of me. I opened the wallet and found not only money, but a passport in the name of a U.S. citizen, Eugene Parta. Only minutes before, Parta had been sitting next to me, looking through Soviet newspapers.

What was I to do? Return the wallet to its owner? What if I was put through another screening? You don't get a pat on the head for breaking the rules. Hand it in to security? If the fellow had dropped the wallet by accident he might be in for some unpleasantness. I decided to return to the library and give the wallet to Parta.

I was rather surprised by the fervor with which Eugene Parta expressed his gratitude, and at the fear on his face when he realized he had dropped his wallet. What I didn't know at the time was that Parta would soon become Max Rallis's deputy and would later replace him as the chief CIA man at Radio Liberty. His appointment was still under consideration on that day, and the loss of his wallet could have had a serious effect on his career.

That was how my acquaintance with Eugene Parta, which was to last almost twenty years, began. When it was needed, I used it to serve my purposes, or rather the purposes of the Soviet state security organs.

George Perry was another in Rallis's department with whom I maintained good relations. A Pole by origin and a former employee of U.S. military intelligence, Perry was eventually kicked out of Radio Liberty for a major error. From time to time he and I would visit the Marine officers' club in Munich, where I enjoyed the agreeable atmosphere only found in elite institutions. As a true patriot of his department for listener research, one day George asked my opinions on a variety of transmissions. I didn't oblige him because it would have been unethical for me, a permanent employee of Liberty, to comment on my colleague's work. It was too much like informing.

George then insisted, "Your opinion would be anonymous. Like one of the many thousands of pieces of a mosaic, so that the final picture is accurate and colorful." I again refused, but in such a way that my response would not offend my friend or break up our relationship.

On one occasion, George asked, "Tell me, Oleg, do you ever meet Soviet citizens?"

"Not likely," I made a dismissive gesture, "I keep clear of them . . . "

"You are making a mistake," Perry said slowly. "Not all of them are working for the KGB. What are you afraid of? We need to know what they think of Liberty's broadcasts. Look, take this questionnaire and if you do meet with any Soviet people, fill it in afterwards. It's best if you can give the exact name, with first name and paternal last name, and if you learn it, the address of your contact. Incidentally, we pay a fee for every completed questionnaire."

I will not say that after that I enthusiastically began questioning Soviet tourists in West Germany, but I did have a few meetings. By introducing myself as a German journalist, and deliberately pronouncing Russian words with a strong accent, I was able to interview a well-known Soviet ice hockey goalkeeper. I asked him to remember any broadcast by Radio Liberty. After thinking long and hard, he couldn't remember one. Even so, I decided that the fact that such a meeting had taken place was reason enough to complete a questionnaire. So I invented a program that the goalkeeper had allegedly listened to, wrote my own opinion of it—which I attributed to him—and added some information about him. The audience research department was delighted, and I was paid a fee of twenty dollars. After that I firmly came to believe that all of the other sources Max Rallis's department had spread around the world did the same as I had done. It was important to get the correct name of, and some information about, the Soviet citizen, then by using a little imagination you could complete the form and come away with twenty dollars in your pocket.

By chance, one day I came across a list of freelance informers engaged in "listener research" that had been carelessly left lying on the desk in George Perry's office. There were about one hundred names on it. There were copying machines in every corridor at Radio Liberty and it took me only a minute to copy the list. They told me that the list was shown to Leonid Brezhnev as evidence that Soviet citizens travelling abroad were being kept under close supervision by the West's special services. It was not for him to complain that the USSR also kept watch on Westerners.

I tried to make use of George Perry to penetrate the secrets of depart-ment "X," which Sergei had asked me about in Karlshorst. I knew from the beginning that I had to move with great caution. There could be no question of inquiring directly, but simply waiting for a convenient opportunity also seemed to be an impermissible luxury. For a start I decided to collect every crumb of information concerning the depart-ment and all of its employees. For a long time, however, I failed to learn anything of importance — only bits of gossip. Both in the old building on Lilienthalstrasse and in the new place on Arabellastrasse, people work-ing in department "X" kept completely to themselves. They avoided making friends, and didn't even use the main canteen.

Chance came to my aid, however, when Willi Klump invited me to a party. I was then going out with Katya, a secretary at Liberty and sister of the famous American movie star Yul Brynner. Everyone was expected to bring something for the table. Willi asked Katya and me to make some *pelmeni*, and another guest, Natasha, to bring some soup. He would provide the vodka. Natasha was secretary to the president of Liberty and her husband, I soon learned, held one of the top jobs in department "X."

His name was Andrei and, to my good fortune, he was a heavy drinker. At the very height of the party, Andrei collapsed on the floor dead drunk. He was taken down to the floor below, to the little room that was once mine, to sleep it off. Some three hours later I went to the room to see how he was.

He opened his eyes and, speaking with difficulty, asked: "Where am I?"

"You are in the next flat. We decided that it would do you no harm to have a little rest."

"Oh dear! That's awkward. I hope I didn't offend anyone."

"Don't worry, everything is alright. Your wife has already gone home, and Willi advises that you spend the night here."

"Oh, the hell with it," he said, and with a feeble wave of the hand went back to sleep.

The next Sunday morning my telephone rang. It was Andrei inviting me to his place for lunch. Natasha, after having laid the table with scrambled eggs with bacon, hot pastries with meat, and a bottle of light wine, went off with the children for a walk. She had hardly closed the door when Andrei firmly pushed the wine aside and with a magician's gesture produced a huge bottle of Smirnoff vodka. He poured two tumblers full to the brim and immediately swigged down half of his. I sipped mine.

"The last time we met I made myself dead drunk," he said guiltily, "and you rescued me. Thank you for that. It is not so very accepted here that people help each other out. To ruin someone . . . oh sure . . . anytime you like. But to help someone selflessly. . . . You are new here and there's a lot you don't know. Shall I tell you about it?"

I raised my glass full of vodka and tapped it against his, but said nothing. With a second swig his glass was completely empty. After that Andrei became very talkative.

"Yes, I got myself drunk," he explained. "But I wasn't risking anything because I was invited by the Americans and it was mostly Americans there—they won't let you down, they understand everything alright. Stick with the Americans and you will have everything. Like me."

He made an expansive gesture, as though he was not living in an ordinary apartment but a huge castle.

"Everything is not so simple, Oleg, as it probably seems to you. Advance yourself while you are still young. Clamber to the top, whatever it may cost you. Work your fingers to the bone, use your elbows and push everyone aside. If you get into difficulties and lose speed, others will immediately take your place—people who are quicker and smarter than you. Then you will have to kowtow to them."

The story of how Andrei landed in the West was typical of those in his generation. In 1942, while fighting on the eastern front in the ranks of the Red Army, Andrei had been taken prisoner by the Germans and placed in a concentration camp. To save himself from almost certain death he agreed to serve in the army of General Vlasov. He was taken prisoner again in Bavaria, but this time by the Americans. It had only been by a miracle that he avoided being deported to Russia. At first, Andrei earned his living as a laborer, then after he learned to type, he joined department "X." Now he was utterly satisfied with his life.

"So you see what happened to me," my new friend continued his lesson. "The Americans liked me and gave me an important job. Listening in! You see . . . "

"They liked me too, apparently. They also took me in. By the way, what do you mean by 'listening in'?"

My question ought not to have put Andrei on his guard, because in that context it did not sound suspicious. Two good friends were having a drink and chatting. Why shouldn't they be interested in each other's affairs?

"Listening in?" Andrei eagerly took the bait. "It's quite elementary! I sit for days on end listening to tape recordings of radio telephone conversations between Soviet military posts. They give me recordings only of particular lines because I know my clients on the other side of the border like my best friends. I can tell their moods by their voices. I know about their problems at work. I know who has been promoted, and to what rank, and who is having trouble. Of course, when it comes to official secrets they prefer to use specially secured lines, but the information we pick up allows the intelligence analyst to learn a great deal. My job is to transcribe what has been recorded on tape and give a short comment."

This lengthy lunch with vodka marked the beginning of our friendship. I was now allowed into the department, where Andrei introduced me to the other employees. Sometimes I invited him to lunch. He became drunk very quickly and then became talkative. It was then not very difficult to get what I needed out of him.

Soon, I knew everyone who worked in department "X." Apart from one blind German they were all countrymen of mine. They received tape recordings from Lamperheim, the location of Radio Liberty's antennas and monitoring station. Department "X" submitted the transcribed texts to a first analysis. Andrei was not exaggerating when he said that he knew a great deal about the Soviet officers whose telephone conversations were listened to month after month, year after year in Lamperheim. The Americans really had this work well organized. The volume of information gathered was enormous. By analyzing and studying it, Radio Liberty people were able to keep tabs on the situation in the Soviet military units located close to the border with NATO. In addition, by listening in on conversations, American intelligence was able to develop fairly good dossiers on many Soviet officers who, unfortunately, were not noted for being careful about what they said over the telephone. I did not forget to emphasize this in my detailed report to the Center.

My report seemed to have been heeded because Andrei began to complain that his job had become more difficult. The Soviets started changing the frequencies without warning, limiting the length of conversations, and using "Aesopian" language more often. I was, of course, pleased at this, although it put the Americans on guard. Department "X" was soon transferred to the Macgrow military intelligence base, which was guarded by marines. The monitoring station was also moved there. Thereafter my contacts with Andrei and his colleagues were more difficult. But I tried for a long time not to lose touch with them.

KGB Versus CIA

The time has now come to turn from the events of my life to Radio Liberty itself.

Most people living in the West have probably never heard of Radio Liberty. But in the Soviet Union, thanks to the propaganda spread about it, Liberty was popular. In the minds of Soviet citizens it was comparable to the CIA, the Pentagon, NATO, international terrorism, world Zionism, ideological conflicts—in short, it was everything that constituted a deadly threat to the existence of the Soviet state. Millions upon millions of rubles were spent to jam Radio Liberty broadcasts. The best Soviet journalists, writers, and television commentators were thrown into the job of compromising the station and its employees. The most popular newspapers regularly branded the personnel of Liberty as "spiders in a tin." Goodness knows how many books were published, films made, and dissertations defended on the subject of Radio Liberty. When I returned to Moscow, out of curiosity, I acquainted myself with this material. From it I got the impression that everything was written by the same person: the facts were identical, and the same examples and names turned up in book after book. Reasoning was often replaced by crude abuse and in general a great deal was turned upside down.

Two journalists who specialized in international affairs for the newspaper *Izvestiya* were particularly successful in this field, and on one occasion they not only succeeded in visiting Radio Liberty offices in Munich, but also managed to exchange words with Robert Redlich, head of the station's department responsible for handling contacts with the press and the public. As I understand it, the conversation was short, and as they say protocolaire. Afterwards, however, the two men from Moscow believed themselves to be real heroes, for they had penetrated the very lair of the enemy! For many years thereafter, they described their "triumph" in newspapers, magazines, and brochures in various ways. They were regularly provided with factual information by the Lubyanka to fuel their stories—compromising stories about people working at Radio Liberty, the latest news about quarrels and events taking place in Munich, and rumors. With this information as a basis, they apparently tapped out appropriate "exposés."

Who read all this stuff? Who ever tried to assess the real effect of the mindless, head-on propaganda campaign? If it had any effect at all, the effect was exactly the opposite of what the Central Committee of the Communist Party had intended. Out of pure curiosity, people tuned their receivers to the Radio Liberty wavelength and tried to make out the voices from Munich through the jamming interference. The more Radio Liberty was attacked by the official authorities, the greater was the interest in its broadcasts. Only a complete idiot could have failed to understand that. And, incidentally, "feeble-minded" would seem to be an indisputable description of the leaders in the Kremlin during the 1970s and 1980s.

I remember expressing doubts about the value of jamming Radio Liberty in one of my reports to the Center. It was an extremely costly operation—the special stations with powerful antennas required such enormous amounts of electrical energy that I heard that the "jammers" in Moscow used all the energy produced by a specially built power station. Just imagine! Those top-secret stations were controlled by thousands of officers, simply to put up a screen to keep news from "over the hill" out. In my report I said that jamming could not be justified either in terms of economics or ideology because the people who wanted to listen to Liberty, *Deutsche Welle*, the Voice of America, the BBC, and other Western radio stations would do so anyway with the help of various tricks. By forbidding people to resort to these sources of information, the regime was only demonstrating its weakness.

When I first sent it, there was no reaction from Moscow to my proposal. Perhaps it had been buried among papers on the desk of some medium-caliber Lubyanka boss. I don't know, but later, in the course of a regular meeting in Karlshorst, when I inquired about the reaction to my proposal, I was advised not to meddle in "things that were not my business" in the future.

That was, as they say, on the one hand. But on the other . . .

The leaders of the Soviet Communist Party and State had good reason to fear Liberty. If anyone knew who the forces behind the facade of the radio station were, and for whom and for what it had been built, it was the leaders of the Soviet Communist Party.

Of course, you can now say what you like about freedom of speech, freedom to spread information, and the free exchange of ideas, but Radio Free Europe and Radio Liberty were products of the Cold War. They were also instruments of "psychological operations" and closely linked with the special services of the United States.

I realize that my vocabulary sounds rather old fashioned and corresponds with the way it is thought proper to discuss these matters today, but why dispense with the truth for the sake of a new political situation?

The truth is this. In the summer of 1950, Radio Free Europe began its broadcast to the countries of Eastern Europe with the following sentence (in Bulgarian, Hungarian, Polish, Czech, Slovak, and Romanian): "We are broadcasting the news—good or bad, but always truthful."

The founding fathers of the new radio station were "private" persons who had set up a "private" organization to deal with the affairs of political refugees from the countries of Eastern Europe. Among these "private" persons were: Dwight D. Eisenhower, Henry Ford the younger, and Nelson Rockefeller; intelligence chiefs Beddel Smith, Allen Dulles, and William Donovan; and other generals, diplomats, and bankers. The collective founder was an organization called the Crusade for Freedom, which later became the National Committee for Free Europe, and still later was known as the Free Europe Committee. The president of the committee, Charles D. Jackson, once said frankly, "We want to create the conditions for the emergence of internal disorder in the countries that our broadcasts reach."

In 1951, U.S. President Harry S. Truman signed a law that provided financing for the activities of "any selected person" from the USSR and the countries of Eastern Europe that supported the postwar tactics and strategies of the United States. All the practical work with émigré organizations was entrusted to the American secret services. Truman's law, numbered one hundred and sixty-five, allotted one hundred million dollars a year for this purpose.

The American intelligence services had no difficulties setting up Radio Free Europe, but it was a different case with Radio Liberty, which was originally called "Liberation."

No matter what the cost, Radio Liberty's organizers wanted it to appear that the idea for the new radio station came entirely from "the emigration from the Soviet Union," and that Liberty was absolutely independent from, and in no way connected to, the intelligence service or with the United States administration. Toward the end of 1948, stories in American newspapers reported that a group of émigrés from Soviet Russia had created an "American Committee for a Free Russia" on December 8, 1948. An appeal by the committee set out its programs. It emphasized that the new organization was a "convinced supporter of democracy in the American, French, and English meaning of the word." It also declared that it refused to collaborate with the groups of Russian émigrés who had disgraced themselves by their "pro-Nazi past."

Right up until 1950, there were no references in the press to the activities of the new organization. Later it reappeared on the political scene, but with a different label—"American Committee for Liberation from Bolshevism." Isaac Don Levine, a major figure in the Zionist movement, who represented the committee, announced: "We are interested only in the creation of a united front for the purposes of anti-Communist propaganda and the campaign against Bolshevism."

It was now a question of combining all who had emigrated—even if they were from the military or ordinary criminals—together on a common platform. There was only one condition governing participation in the "anti-Bolshevik campaign" (and in a share in the funds set aside by the Truman law no. 165), it was: unconditional recognition by everyone of the leading role played by the U.S. Department of State, or more precisely its special services.

In March 1953, Radio Liberty (then known as "Liberation") began broadcasting to the Soviet Union. The new radio station was registered as "private and noncommercial" and described itself as "the voice of former Soviet citizens appealing to its former fellow countrymen from abroad." Recordings of those early transmissions have not been preserved in the Radio Liberty archives, but I have been told that each broadcast began with the ticking of a metronome followed by the voice of the announcer saying: "Today, the—th of March 1953, Joseph Stalin has lived for so many years, months, days, and hours. It is now—o'clock in Moscow. Radio 'Liberation' now begins its transmission."

Stalin died on the fifth of March. All sorts of stories about this are told in Radio Liberty. Some seriously believed that the radio station speeded the dictator's end.

In the mid-1950s, representatives of the so-called postwar emigration began to be drawn into work for Radio Liberty—for example, members of the committee of people who had fought with General Vlasov, of the Anti-Bolshevik Union of Crimean Tatars, and the Union for the Liberation of the Peoples of Russia, (people who had actively collaborated with the Nazis during the Second World War). In this way the first declaration issued by the "American Committee for a Free Russia" was finally consigned to oblivion. People in the intelligence service given the task of recruiting staff found a shortage of able and "clean" émigrés who were capable of playing the role of propagandists. It was then that they decided to close their eyes to the shameful past of the majority of members of the "postwar emigration."

The aim justified the means. And the aim was a grandiose one—the total elimination of communism.

Thus elderly monarchists from noble Russian families, and semi-literate Vlasov supporters with no family all found themselves in the same boat. Members of the Jewish intelligentsia who had escaped from the USSR found themselves working alongside former Nazi policemen who had taken part in the extermination of Jews. There were convinced fighters against Bolshevism along with "displaced persons" without any precise political views. And, if not to reconcile, at least to suppress the contradictions within this variegated collection of people and make it pull in the same direction, the Americans resorted to a well-proven device: they paid all the employees of Radio Liberty very well. They were not only paid a great deal, they were paid much more than journalists who worked for American or German radio stations.

For instance, in the 1980s, my annual pay amounted to one hundred and fifty thousand German Marks, which was more than a minister in the government of Bavaria received. Yet I did not belong to the category of the most highly paid employees. At the beginning of my career I received nine hundred and eight Marks a month. That now seems a small salary, but in those days it was possible to buy a quite decent lunch in our canteen for one Mark.

Money, free accommodations, villas, privileged treatment regarding taxes, profitable insurance plans—all these benefits bound people tightly to their new job, made them completely forget former sympathies or antipathies, kept mouths shut, and provided the incentive for employees to carry out, without question, any order. That's the way it was then, and that's the way it is today. And if the employees of Radio Liberty continue to campaign energetically for the preservation of Liberty—although it has now fulfilled its task—it is primarily out of fear of losing a well-paid job. The majority of them would not find work like that elsewhere.

The American committee and its branches—Radio Liberty and Radio Free Europe—were able to acquire substantial financial resources because of the new president of the committee, Hoyland Sargent. They could not have found a better man for the job. He was young and full of ambitious plans. Having at one time been an assistant secretary of state, he had good connections with the upper levels of the administration. And, he knew his way around the world of special services because he had once headed the commission on technical-industrial espionage in the U.S. Army.

In the early 1950s, the first directives were drawn up to guide the work of Radio Liberty. Although they were subsequently changed and extended, they remained essentially the same. They might be summarized in the following way. Employees of the radio station must do everything to ensure that their broadcasts were not identified by the listeners with the Americans and especially not with the CIA. The radio station must earn and maintain a reputation that did not give rise to doubts as to its honesty and reliability. The station had to create in its listeners the image of "a guest in the home," which meant employing a friendly tone, avoiding aggressiveness, and not including in broadcasts unverified or doubtful information. All broadcasts ought to end with the posing of a question. The more striking and unpleasant the facts, the less emotion there should be in the program. Broadcasters must not use language that demeaned Soviet listeners. They should avoid engaging in polemics with the Soviet media. And so forth. The ensuing directives took up fifty pages of typescript when written out in detail. The principal aim of Radio Liberty was to shake the listeners' faith in Communist ideology, put a grain of doubt and discontent in their minds, and prepare the ground for the overthrow of the existing regime.

In addition to the directives, Sargent devised a series of measures that provided severe sanctions for the publication of information about the sources of Radio Liberty and Radio Free Europe finances. On March 15, 1971, *The New York Times* wrote about these measures:

"Sooner or later all employees of Radio Free Europe and Radio Liberty will be obliged to sign a document saying: 'I, the undersigned, have been informed that the radio stations are a branch of the CIA and that the CIA provides funds to maintain the organization. . . . In the event of this information being passed to third parties the person responsible exposes himself to a fine of up to ten thousand dollars or imprisonment for up to ten years."

In my time employees did not sign such documents. The beginning of my active employment by Soviet intelligence coincided with an almighty scandal that flared up across the ocean about the links between Radio Liberty and Radio Free Europe and the American special services.

Here I can reveal yet another secret: The KGB stirred up the trouble by dropping strictly factual material about the work of Radio Liberty and Radio Free Europe in the right places. Although they did not succeed in their principal goal—closing down the radio stations—the KGB certainly got on the nerves of American intelligence.

It all started in January 1971 with an announcement to correspondents by Clifford Case, the Republican senator from the state of New Jersey, that over a period of twenty years the CIA had spent several hundred million dollars supporting Radio Liberty and Radio Free Europe. For the average person this was like having a bucket of ice-cold water poured over him because until then nobody had known that the émigré radio stations were secretly being financed by the U.S. government. On January 25, Case spoke at a meeting of the Senate Committee on Foreign Affairs. He did not demand the immediate cessation of the radio stations' activities, or threaten to leave them without financing, but he did ask that they be placed under the control of the Congress and that they be included "in the process of the distribution of resources carried out by Congress."

Every scandal has a tendency to work itself out, and so it was with this one. The press, having had its fill of criticizing the CIA, gradually forgot about émigré radio stations situated in far-away Europe. But Moscow did not sit idly by. On March 9, 1971, a news agency reported the return to Warsaw of an officer, Andrei Chekhovich, who had for several years worked for Radio Free Europe and had carried out a special task for Polish intelligence. He spoke at a press conference about his revelations, after which the fuss around the radio stations gathered new force.

On May 24, 1971, a session of the Senate Foreign Affairs Committee met in Washington with only one item on its agenda — public financing of Radio Free Europe and Svoboda. At the outset everything went smoothly, with speakers expressing their thoughts about the new system of financing. After a representative of the Department of State had spoken, however, the chairman of the committee, William Fulbright, intervened in the discussion. He demanded in very sharp terms recognition of the direct links between the CIA and the radio stations and said that in his opinion the stations' activities were not in accord with the administration's statements about its desire to improve relations with the Soviet Union and the countries of Eastern Europe.

A bill that provided for the creation of a special corporation, "not subject to taxation and not profit making," was submitted for the Senate committee's consideration. The State Department and the CIA intended that the corporation would finance and supervise the two radio stations. Some senators, including Fulbright, spoke against the bill. The question of the American Council for Private International Communications, and the question of the size of the subsidies to the radio stations, were debated until the end of 1971. Finally, in the beginning of December, the House of Representatives voted by a majority of two hundred and seventy-one to twelve to allot the two stations "as an exceptional measure" 74.5 million dollars for the next two years. The Senate restricted financing of the radio stations in 1972, allotting them thirty-six million dollars.

Another stage in the affair came in February 1972, when Senator Fulbright sent President Nixon a memorandum. In it he again returned to the details of the discussion about émigré radio stations and stated his position quite unambiguously.

"The senators will probably recall," Fulbright said, "that these stations were financed by 'collections among schoolchildren,' at least that is what we were told for many years. But it turned out that those 'collections' amounting to hundreds of millions of dollars were actually provided by the CIA and were part of a piece of deception aimed at persuading American taxpayers, as well as the peoples of Eastern Europe, that the radio stations were private organizations depending only on private contributions.

"The radio stations Radio Free Europe and Radio Liberty were simply part of a system—a system of lies and deception, a system of plots—aimed at misleading not only the American people but anyone who was ready to listen.

"Independently of what labels these radio stations go under, the situation is such that this activity, even if it includes nothing but 'broadcasting the bare facts,' gives rise to a series of foreign policy problems, including what is by no means the least important question of the extent of our interference in the internal political affairs of other countries . . .

"Mister President!" Fulbright appealed to President Nixon. "I consider that these radio stations should be given the opportunity to occupy a worthy place in the graveyard of relics of the Cold War."

How did the President react? Initially, if my memory serves me well, he preferred to stand on the sidelines and avoided making any comments. But at the most decisive moment Nixon took a determined stand in defense of the "relics of the Cold War." He announced that he was deeply concerned at the possibility of closing down the radio stations and that it would be a tragedy if they did not continue their work.

It is interesting to note that some deputies to the West German Bundestag joined in the demands that the stations be closed. On March 23, 1972, they sent a telegram to the West German chancellor and to the American president recommending that the U.S. Congress stop financing the radio stations and cancel their broadcast license. Both individuals and whole organizations joined in the protest movement against the presence of Radio Free Europe and Radio Liberty on German territory.

It must be pointed out that many Germans, and especially the professional journalists, looked upon the employees of the émigré radio stations with distaste. They knew that we were working at the behest of the CIA and that we all bore the American stigma.

You can imagine the situation we were in in Munich when the fate of Radio Free Europe and Radio Liberty was being argued in Washington. There were occasions when employees at the stations were not paid their salaries for months on end. No one was sure what the next day would bring. Depression and uncertainty prevailed. There were rumors that the American administration was looking to transfer both stations to another country—there was talk of Spain or Portugal, where Radio Liberty and Radio Free Europe had their own aerials, and of Belgium, where NATO headquarters were located. The rumors were not groundless: Washington considered moving the stations, but all three countries flatly refused to receive the multicolored band of anti-Communists.

Apart from purely political considerations, I believe a feeling of plain distaste played a role in this.

The whole affair came to an end in December 1973, when the two radio stations were removed from direct control of the CIA. Supervision of their activities and their financing was now to be carried out by governmental bodies of the United States through the so-called Council for International Broadcasting, which did not mean, of course, that American intelligence had departed from us altogether. The top jobs in Liberty and Free Europe continued to be taken by Americans connected in one way or another with the special services. But all secret matters were more carefully disguised.

After these sensational events nobody had any doubts about whose offspring the Munich stations were. Newspapers in the United States and Europe said openly that both Liberty and Free Europe were primarily "covers" for the American intelligence services, offering a good opportunity for the legal concealment of secret operations and also a source for the recruitment of agents and regular supplies of necessary information. If you are not too idle to find the *Encyclopedia of American Intelligence and Espionage* (J. A. O'Tool, 1988) and open it to page three hundred and eighty-two, you can read about all this in great detail.

In this connection I want once again to stress that I was not working against the émigrés or the radio stations, but against the American intelligence services, which were in turn working against my country.

Not every employee of Liberty and Free Europe was involved in dirty business. I knew many who, for decades, dutifully came to work without having the slightest idea about the presence of the secret service next to them. Moreover, there were worthy people, especially among the émigrés of the "first wave," who would never have agreed to have anything to do with spying. The very thought of it was hateful to them. Having been brought up in the spirit of crystalline honesty, high morals, and having taken in with their mother's milk their conception of honor and dignity, they would sooner have died from hunger than have entered into any collaboration with the special services. For such people a job in Liberty really offered an opportunity to conduct an honest and friendly conversation with their fellow countrymen.

But by the end of the 1960s, there were very few representatives of the old emigration left. Liberty was in great need of younger people who had good knowledge about the Soviet Union, were familiar with the journalist's trade, and would be able to accept the "rules of the game." Where were they to be found? There was only one place in the West—Israel, which was receiving a steady stream of "fresh" people from the USSR.

After some hesitation, the men in charge of the radio stations decided to recruit new employees there. In the mid-1970s, I was involved in this: I travelled to Israel five times, sometimes with a girlfriend, visiting all parts of the country and making contacts. In Tel-Aviv, I got to know the candidates, had discussions with them, and recommended the best for permanent jobs.

At the same time I informed the Center that such a personnel policy for the radio station would inevitably produce big problems. By then I already had a good idea of the internal affairs of Liberty, sensed the mood of the various groups, and could see behind the external well-being a concealed hostility that never relaxed, not even for an hour.

A Delayed-Action Mine

I have said that the Americans were in complete command of nearly a thousand employees in Radio Liberty and had found remarkable ways of doing it. Nevertheless, the contradictions that remained among the absolutely different kinds of people broke through to the surface. That is what happened, for example, in the second half of 1975, when an "Open Letter" served as the spark that ignited a big scandal. It was written by an announcer, Victoria Semenova, and addressed to the head of the Russian program, John Lodezen. Semenova complained that, in her view, there was a lack of "Russian spirit" in Radio Liberty's programs and that the editor-in-chief, Vladimir Matusevich, was flatly opposed to the whole idea of a "Russian spirit."

"I will define what I mean by the 'Russian spirit,'" Victoria Semenova wrote. "It is primarily a love of Russia and the Russian people. It means suffering, protest, and grief concerning all who are tormented and persecuted. It means belonging to the great Russian culture and being indignant at its destruction by the Communist experiment." She asked Mr. Lodezen why Radio Liberty did not broadcast programs for Russia and the Russian people.

For the uninitiated it was impossible to understand what was behind this letter and the great fight that developed afterwards into open confrontation and conclusion in the courts. In my view the situation was explained best by a veteran Radio Liberty employee, Timothy Kiverov, whose letter in support of Semenova read:

"The interests of the United States of America, represented by the

American administration of Radio Liberty, of the various national programmes and of the Russian program cannot always be coordinated. It is quite understandable that the American management must first of all protect and express the interests of the USA in a frequently discordant choir. I give the American administration its due for the efforts it has made—with difficulty—to coordinate what cannot be coordinated. Its efforts were worthy of the most sincere recognition on the part of the Russians. One wants to point out, for example, the considerable success the management had in reconciling the differences between the 'old' and the 'new' émigrés in the 1950s and 1960s. . . . Again, an unquestionable success on the part of Liberty was the influence its broadcasts had on the emigration of Jews to Israel. The radio station devoted a great deal of attention to this question and supported many in their efforts to leave the USSR. But then there took place a tragic coincidence, which although unavoidable, could have been foreseen.

"The Jewish emigration from the USSR offered the possibility of rejuvenating the radio station with new cultural forces. . . . But the rejuvenation was carried out in a strangely hurried manner, the results of which we can see today.

"The staff of the radio station was joined by people who had been brought up in a country cut off for fifty years from real human thought and taught political and moral views produced by the Communist Party. The majority of these people turned out to be under the influence of what modern psychologists call the 'prodigal son' complex. The mental state of such people is very complicated and painful. Employees of the radio station noticed immediately that the new people kept to themselves and were distrustful of others and even hostile. The American management, which had in the past been so successful in reconciling the differences, for some reason this time took the side of the new people, especially in the Russian program. Sad to say, the general level of the transmissions began to decline rapidly.

"It is not without interest," Kiverov wrote, "to note that the domination of the Russian program by new employees immediately gave rise to a whole series of conflicts. The majority of the people, who had so unexpectedly found themselves in conditions of freedom and kindness, were for the time being able to use those conditions for doing things that it would be difficult to describe as kindly."

You can imagine how the Center needed this! A good deal of material came into their hands for possible use as counter-propaganda. The Lubyanka got to know all there was to know about every new employee of Radio Liberty—their weaknesses and their psychological and mental state—and could forecast with great accuracy what the new arrivals would do in a given situation. The Americans were not, of course, in a position to do that. Without realizing what they were doing, they had placed a delayed-action mine beneath the radio station. They had done it themselves—the KGB had not moved a finger.

At the time I was responsible for the first half-hour of broadcasting in each hour of broadcasts in Russian. That meant that commentaries and reviews were based on the latest news. All directives about how to treat events in the USSR and the world, which came from the top people in Radio Liberty and directly from Washington, landed immediately on my desk. It was extremely important material and it helped analysts at the Center forecast with great accuracy the twists and turns of the current foreign policy of the United States.

With the situation in the Russian service becoming explosive, creating the possibility of punitive measures by the administration, Moscow categorically forbade me to get involved. I did, however, have to send a regular account of what was happening. Moscow followed attentively as the quarrel gathered strength and, I believe, regularly threw its own logs on the fire.

I could not, of course, be absolutely neutral. It would have meant losing friends and the authority I enjoyed. So I adopted a position that I still hold today. In summary, my position was as follows. Any inflaming of national passions is wrong. Any extolling of one nation or humiliation of another is wrong. Efforts to stir up national antagonism or racial hatred, which in West Germany are criminal offenses, must be dealt with. The campaign of slander against particular employees of national programs and against the whole of the Russian program serves only to compromise Radio Liberty in the eyes of the United States Congress. Such a campaign is, however, a welcome gift to Soviet propaganda, which has long depicted the employees of Radio Liberty as "spiders in a tin."

That was roughly the spirit that reigned in my apartment when a group of employees drafted a memorandum concerning the management of the radio station. It turned out that, contrary to the instructions from the Center, I had gotten myself involved in the quarrel.

Preparation of the memorandum had been preceded by the arrival and speech to members of the Ukrainian and Russian departments by a "fresh" dissident from the USSR, Leonid Plyush, a person of extreme right-wing nationalist views. The extremists in both of our hostile camps, it appeared, where simply waiting for this. Plyush's speech served to set off a fresh outburst of passions. The situation became more dangerous. After that, the "third emigration" went over to a determined attack. That was why the collective memorandum was born in my apartment. In it we asked that the management of Radio Liberty take decisive steps to put an end to the slander and provocation and restore a friendly atmosphere to the radio station.

By the morning of January 18, 1977, the memorandum was ready. We then began to collect signatures. Altogether about seventy people signed, not only people from the Russian department but also from the Armenian, Georgian, Tadzhik, Belorussian, and Azerbaijanian desks. . . . The result was a very impressive document that, as we had expected, made an impression on the American management.

An immediate diplomatic reply from the vice president of Radio Liberty/Radio Free Europe, Walter Scott, followed. Addressing both the warring sides simultaneously, Scott appealed to them to come to terms and stop their mutual squabbling. Otherwise, he warned, there could be serious consequences for the radio station. After that, at a brief conference, the initiators of the memorandum decided to accept Scott's arguments and in the future to do nothing that would worsen the situation. This actually corresponded with the position that we had set out in our memorandum.

But the other party decided to continue the confrontation. They brought an action in the German court accusing all the signatories of anti-Semitism and other grave offenses.

With obvious reluctance, the court heard the case. The litigation dragged on for a long time, only ending when the parties withdrew their accusations and agreed to be reconciled.

The quarrel, which went on for several years, was objectively to the benefit of Moscow. The "conspiracy of silence" around Radio Liberty was again upset and details of the squabble were seized on by the Western media. The Soviet newspapers were assured of first-class material for a long time. Interestingly, the West German press frequently referred to them when writing about events in Munich.

Again there were questions to American Congressmen, commissions were set up to study the work of the two radio stations, and some heads rolled at the CIA.

Later some of the recent emigrants from Israel (including some who were taken on with my help), because of the memorandum, counted me in the camp of the anti-Semites. I can be reproached for many things but not that. Even if I had wanted to become an extremist in some field, my bosses in Moscow would have found an opportunity to cut such a desire off at the root. Otherwise they would have called me home immediately.

Unlike the majority of employees I did not belong to any political or national group. I was not an old émigré, or a Vlasov man, or a Jew. I had not had a dissident past in the USSR. I had not been through the Nazi camps. I had not been a "displaced person." I was simply a former sailor and a fugitive. The only one of its kind. As time went on I learned to extract some benefit from that too. The fact was that, from the very beginning, there had been rumors about why I was in Munich. One was that I was connected to American intelligence, which explained why I had been taken on at the radio station. I made no great effort to refute that claim once I saw the servile way that most of the staff behaved toward the Americans. What was most surprising was that the Americans were also apparently suited by my status as a man who kept to himself, was not especially close to anyone, and did not depend on anyone. In any case, the management of Radio Liberty did a great deal that helped me to succeed in my career. As with any other management (whether in the USA or in the USSR) what was needed for the middle rank of managerial jobs was not especially talented personnel, but reliable and tested "work horses." That is exactly what I was in the eyes of the Americans.

In the course of the twenty years working at Liberty, sometimes jumping up two rungs of the administrative ladder at once, I managed to rise as far as the chief editor of the Russian Program. That meant I had reached the ceiling for a person who was not a citizen of the United States.

In May 1986, after my return to the USSR, Vladimir Maximov, a Russian author who lived in Paris, accused, in an open letter to U.S. President Ronald Reagan, those in charge of Radio Liberty of taking an unprofessional approach to the appointment of staff. In his familiar energetic and abrupt style, Maximov inquired of the President:

" . . . for what services and by virtue of what professional or business qualities does a man who was only yesterday a rank-and-file seaman in the Soviet merchant navy, who is incapable of arranging words in a literate manner in the most elementary Russian sentence, and who is from morning in a state of permanent delirium, get appointed to deliver final judgment on the work of doctors of science, qualified specialists in all fields of Soviet life, experienced journalists of many years standing, authors, and other people concerned with the arts and science with Russian and sometimes worldwide reputations?

"The answer to this question suggests itself. Being professional bureaucrats with all the qualities derived from that—intolerance of other people's and especially émigrés' opinions, a ridiculous self-confidence and an incurable inferiority complex, which they try to sublimate, humiliating subordinates who depend upon them materially—these people regard any manifestation of independent thought, personality or creative effort in a person as a challenge and a threat to their own comfortable existence. For this reason they select staff who correspond to their own intellectual and professional level."

Perhaps Vladimir Yemelyanovich Maximov was right, by and large. But we live in a world of real people and concrete circumstances.

I behaved exactly as was required in order to be on good terms with the bosses of Radio Liberty and, by so doing, carry out as best I could the tasks set by Soviet intelligence. As for my illiteracy, I will leave that accusation to the author's conscience. Especially since Maximov himself, as far as I know, has not graduated from any institutions of higher education.

The feuding at Radio Liberty, which I have described, was certainly encouraged by the anonymous letters and leaflets signed by the so-called Russian nationalists, which sometimes appeared in the radio station. Their openly extreme nationalist content did nothing to promote reconciliation, but on the contrary provided our opponents with fresh trump cards.

"Aha!" they would say. "Now you are showing your true face. You are all just disguised pogrom leaders!" Later, it was rumored at the station that the letters and leaflets were the work of the KGB, which was interested in having everyone at odds with each other.

I was amazed when, some years later, quite by accident I discovered who those "Russian nationalists" were. They turned out to be a single individual, the old carpenter Voychevsky. He had once served as a captain in the "white" Cossack army, and during the Second World War had fought on Hitler's side in the units commanded by Ataman Krasnov. He then worked for Radio Liberty as a carpenter until he was pensioned off. Shortly before his death this former captain invited me to buy some orders and medals from the Civil War. I went to his little apartment on the Opalstrasse. After inviting me to the table with a samovar and some bread rolls, Voychevsky got down to business.

"The doctors have passed a death sentence on me," the old soldier said. "Cancer. I haven't very long to live. Out of a desire to help my wife arrange a decent funeral for me I have decided to sell off some of my archives and things."

With those words he handed me a big box of papers, old newspaper clippings and decorations. The Cossack wanted three thousand Marks for the lot. Without bargaining and without paying much attention to the contents I picked up the box and left.

A few days later Voychevsky died. When I came to sort out the things I had bought, I came across some typewritten drafts and different versions of those letters by the Russian nationalists. After that there could be no further doubt—the author of the provocative proclamations was none other than the old Cossack.

But he had never worked for the KGB.

Spies Everywhere

Although it was still a long time before my regularly scheduled meeting, I received a signal that I was to go immediately to Karlshorst. This happened very rarely.

Somewhat puzzled, I flew to Berlin. The conversation with my immediate superior was short. It concerned a new Radio Liberty employee—a subordinate of mine in the department of the Russian service of Liberty. He had been born in a European country, of which he remained a citizen, spoke several languages very well, including Russian, and had a questionable character and big ambitions. It seemed to me that he had deliberately chosen to work for Radio Liberty because of the station's reputation for harboring spies and was anxious to offer his services in that regard. It was obvious that he had connections with the NTS and that he was extremely interested in the ongoing squabbles concerning the Russian Orthodox Church.

I had already written and sent a background paper about this man to the Center. Never thinking that such an ordinary report, of which I had sent a great many, would evoke this kind of reaction, I then forgot about it.

In Karlshorst, after detailed questioning about this new man, the officer from Moscow said, "You see, Oleg, this fellow has already been to see us in the Lubyanka and expressed a desire to collaborate. We lost track of him. Now he has turned up again."

The officer further explained that upon his arrival as a tourist in Moscow, my new colleague had been caught handing a Soviet citizen a miniature film that contained instructions that the NTS and the Vatican's secret service had asked him to deliver. The KGB must have had its own people in the Vatican because the "tourist" was kept under observation almost from the moment he deplaned and set foot in Moscow. After being caught in the act and arrested, he was threatened with a trial and several years in a camp. Faced with the gloomy prospect of imprisonment, the "tourist" prepared a letter that he entitled "Proposal for Collaboration with the Soviet Intelligence Service." Yes, that is precisely what he called it; I saw the original in Karlshorst.

In this letter the "tourist" confirmed what he had already admitted under interrogation—that he had contacts with anti-Soviet centers—and proposed that he should be allowed to penetrate more deeply into the leadership of those centers. He gave a detailed description of the secret department of the so-called Russian Catholic seminary in Rome—which, according to him, prepared priests for subversive activities within the territory of the USSR. And, he described how communications were maintained between that department and its people in the Soviet Union.

"I could try to find out the names of the foreigners who come to the USSR to make contact with the Uniates," the tourist suggested, "as well as the names of those Soviet citizens in holy orders (and some who are not) who maintain contacts with agents of the Vatican contrary to the interests of the Soviet state."

The "tourist" described the Modesto monastery in Milan as "a clandestine center for meetings between Vatican agents and their handlers," and suggested, "I could also penetrate more deeply into the NTS, but I admit that would be more difficult. I do not yet know how the NTS will react to the news of my arrest and possible release. I could tell them that the Soviet authorities arrested me for breaking some currency or customs regulation or for having an anti-Soviet conversation with the person who reported me to the KGB."

What people will do to save their own skins! Clearly, fear of the Siberian camps was strong because the "tourist" further suggested in his "proposal" that: "In order to provide the Soviet authorities with a guarantee that I will carry out their instructions I am ready to be compromised here in Moscow—in a way that will cause me serious difficulties in Europe. I am sure that Soviet intelligence is in a position to do this, while I, conscious of my guilt in the eyes of the Soviet authorities, am ready to do anything it deems necessary."

The Soviet authorities decided that it was best to release the "tourist" and allow him to go wherever he pleased. Perhaps the KGB had placed some hopes in him, but now in Karlshorst I set about disappointing my Moscow colleagues.

"Your potential agent is obviously psychologically unbalanced," I said after reading his "proposal." "He is too ambitious and also extremely cowardly. Apart from that, there is something not right about his family life. In my opinion he is someone who is ready to work for any special service if it is to his benefit, even for the devil himself. I would not be in the least surprised if one day similar "proposals" were found in the safes of other intelligence services."

The officer from Moscow was very disheartened. He had not expected such a strong opinion from me. I understood that the people in the Lubyanka wanted to acquire another source inside the anti-Soviet centers, but this "tourist" struck me as far too doubtful a character. A spy does not have to be virtuous, but it is better to avoid such anomalous types. I never knew what Moscow's final decision was—whether they turned down his offer or whether, ignoring me, they worked with him.

I have recounted this episode for two reasons. First, because there are numerous documents like the "Proposal for Collaboration" preserved in the KGB archives. I have seen some of them, and I know about others from my colleagues. The files containing such papers are marked "preserve indefinitely." If any were made public, citizens of Russia would learn quite a few interesting tidbits about many so-called dissidents and freedom fighters. The archives contain their signed denunciations of each other, their signed agreements to collaborate secretly with the KGB, and other compromising materials.

I am not in favor of declassifying material of this kind. In our broken and confused society there are enough insults, quarrels, and misunderstandings. Why add to them? It would serve no purpose. Man is weak, and in his desire to survive, to save his skin, to avoid repressive measures, or to go abroad he will sometimes engage in treachery or ruin his neighbor. Moreover, the security organs had many devices for breaking even the strongest individuals. As for the weak ones I will say nothing—they were scared stiff at the mere mention of the Lubyanka. It is not their fault, but a misfortune, that they signed such papers.

Second, at times I felt that there were only two kinds of people working at Radio Liberty and Radio Free Europe—agents of the CIA and agents of the KGB. Much has been written about the activities of the American intelligence services—even in the West. Their involvement with the radio station is a generally recognized fact and to try to prove it again is, as they say, pushing at an open door. But the special services of the countries of Eastern Europe were also active. Until 1971, for instance, Polish counterintelligence received regular reports from Captain Andrei Chekhovich, an employee of Radio Free Europe. When he returned to Warsaw he was replaced by Mechislav Lakh. The Bulgars had the services of an officer of their state security, Khristo Khristov, and the Czechoslovaks set up Pavel Minarik in Munich. And those are only the ones whose names were revealed and appeared in the press.

Employees of Radio Liberty were often involuntary witnesses to complicated, unexplainable stories. On one occasion, for instance, a visitor from the Soviet Union, Vladimir Zlatkin, turned up in Paris. At one time he had been a correspondent for the major news agency APN and, of course, a member of the Soviet Communist Party. Zlatkin had married a Frenchwoman in Moscow and brought her with him to live in Paris. What do you know! A member of the CPSU married to a French Communist, a man carrying a red Soviet passport, was hired by Liberty and made director of the Paris office. After that, many people were convinced that the KGB already had its people at the highest level of Radio Liberty management.

Although Vladimir Zlatkin was a very hard working, capable man, practically every employee of the Paris office rose against him. I got to know him in Munich, where he went to introduce the writer Vladimir Maximov. One year later Zlatkin was suddenly thrown out of Liberty without any explanation. He was sacked and that was that. Again everyone was lost in conjecture: What had happened?

Sometime later I met him in Paris. He was in a bad way: His wife was selling newspapers and Vladimir was still unemployed.

"I just don't understand," he told me. "Everybody thinks I am a KGB agent."

All traces of him soon vanished. Interestingly, for a long time my bosses at the Center continued to be interested in Vladimir—his financial state, his general condition, and his plans, but when I tried to find out who he really was, I could never tell by my colleagues' behavior whether they knew anything or whether Zlatkin was as much of a mystery to them as he was to me.

I knew a number of people who were well liked by everybody at Radio Liberty, but carried the secret of their many years of collaboration with the Soviet KGB with them to the grave. I also know that our people are still there to this day. "A holy place is never empty."

Why, if communism no longer exists, do the broadcasts of Radio Liberty continue from German, and now from Russian, soil under the supervision of the American intelligence service, with funds from the United States? What role does Radio Liberty now play? Does it tell the citizens of the former Soviet Union about their life? We now have a level of freedom of speech as was never dreamed of in the West.

Would the Americans like it if Russia opened a radio station in Cuba and invited people who had emigrated from the United States (there are not many, but there are some in Russia) to work in it; filled the office with active and retired employees of the state security service; and began broadcasting in English to the whole of America—allegedly for the purpose of spreading objective information? The very idea of such a thing seems absurd, doesn't it? Yet the situation with Radio Liberty is now precisely that.

So why should the Lubyanka have to withdraw its people from Munich?

No, only parity will do! Only mutual and identical steps on both sides. As for the American intelligence service, there are no signs that its activities against the former Soviet Union have diminished. I understand the thinking of the top people at Langley: they are worried about what is taking place in Russia and want to keep the situation under control because they are, above all, concerned with the interests of their own state. It is also possible that some in the United States would like to influence the situation in such a way as to break up Russia and render it a powerless, backward, impoverished third world country for many years to come. Secret intelligence operations are irreplaceable for such purposes.

In the autumn of 1992, the *Independent Newspaper*, which is published in Moscow, printed a letter from Munich signed by someone named Yevgenya Nikolayev—a name that means nothing to me. The author heatedly demanded that the activities of KGB agents in Radio Liberty be immediately exposed. He asserted that it was on KGB operatives' instructions that, in the summer of 1992, the people in charge of Liberty closed down the "samizdat department" and dismissed several former Soviet political prisoners, so that they "could not in future contribute to the liberation of Russia from communism and Communists."

The "closing down of the 'samizdat department' and the dismissal of the former political prisoners cannot be explained only by reference to the stupidity of the American management. It can be regarded, I repeat, as a success for the subversive activity of the KGB in Radio Liberty"— this was the conclusion drawn by Nikolayev. At the end of his letter, Nikolayev proposed that an investigation into the subversive activities of the KGB in Radio Liberty be undertaken; that a list of the KGB employees who had been introduced into Liberty be published in Russia; and that a list of the employees of the American administration of Liberty whom the KGB men had managed to suborn be published.

The fact that this letter was printed indicates that either the editors of the *Independent Newspaper* had swallowed the bait of some schizophrenic, or that the letter had been written by someone in the Lubyanka to stir up distrust among employees of the radio station toward the

Americans working there and to start them quarrelling among themselves. (KGB officers have always been great masters in the art of disinformation, of compromising people they don't like, and of creating conflicts.)

In the mid-1970s the lads in the Lubyanka had managed, through a third person, to sell one of the volumes of a secret publication that contained lists of people sought by the security service to an American intelligence agent. The volume, which was always kept up to date by the KGB, sold for a large sum. It contained the following information about me:

"Tumanov, Oleg Alexandrovich; born 1944; born and lived in Moscow; Russian; secondary education; formerly a candidate for membership in the CPSU; draftsman by profession; served as a seaman in a military unit of the Baltic fleet. Height 173 centimeters, dark hair, oval face, blue eyes, three birthmarks on right cheek near temple. Father—Tumanov Alexander Vasilevich, mother—Tumanova Yevdokiya Andreyevna, brother— Tumanov Igor Alexandrovich, close relationship with Danilova Tatyana Konstantinovna. They live in Moscow.

"On the night of November 18, 1965, when his ship lay at anchor in the territorial waters of the United Arab Republic in the bay of Salum 1.5 kilometers from the shore, he disappeared. He was found to be living in Munich and working in the news department of Radio Liberty under the name of Valeri Shulgin. Gives regular anti-Soviet talks.

"A warrant for his arrest was approved by the military procurator of the Baltic fleet. There is a photograph of him taken in 1965 and a sample of his handwriting.

"The file on his case is with the KGB directorate for Moscow and the Moscow region. (Previously reported missing by the KGB and listed as number 27 for 1966, number 13 in the file.)"

This description contains three major errors. First, my eyes are not blue, they're green. Second, my mother's maiden name is not Andreyevna, but Andrianovna. And finally, I have only one birthmark on my right cheek—certainly not three. This is a typical example of a purely Russian attitude to world affairs—errors even in such important matters as the search for a major criminal.

But that is not the essence of the affair. The KGB was quite successful in obtaining what it wanted. The Americans believed that their agent had made a good deal, and were delighted to find my name in the book— which helped to convince them once again of my loyalty. But there was no other useful information in it. They already had detailed dossiers on all the people listed in the book and had put them through the "filters" of their screening and rescreening processes. Having quickly realized this, the people from Langley gave the book to the NTS, permitting them to publish the lists of people sought by the KGB in *Posev* magazine. Although NTS was probably motivated by the best of intentions, publication of the lists provoked panic among the émigrés, many of whom had things to conceal in their past—criminal activities, collaborations with the Nazis, and informing on people, for example. The KGB's secret book, which was strictly intended for official use, elaborated their histories in detail. Some of the active participants in the anti-Soviet movement, who had carefully nursed irreproachable reputations, now felt as if they were standing naked in a busy square.

There was also panic at Radio Liberty. The lists in *Posev* included quite a few employees of the radio station, both old and new. Some—like me—brushed it all contemptuously aside: We knew these KGB tricks. Most, however, were really frightened.

And that was all that Moscow needed.

The "Apostle"

The KGB is a very big organization. It has, with good reason, sometimes been called a state within a state. The largest, most powerful, most prestigious, and most secret directorate in the KGB was the First Chief Directorate—the organization responsible for foreign intelligence. The entire town of Yasenevo, located just outside the ring road near Moscow, was built to house this directorate. It is surrounded with a double concrete wall and barbed wire and is carefully guarded. At the gate is a sign that reads "Scientific Research Center."

The greater part of the First Directorate was housed in Yasenevo. The town's vast territory was not, however, sufficient to accommodate an intelligence school, a center for the training of terrorist and subversive groups, and some operational units, which were spread around the Moscow region. The extent of the real might of the First Directorate was known, I believe, only to a few highly placed individuals in the top ranks of the KGB. In Yasenevo, along with the services directing the activity of Soviet agents throughout the world, there was also a research institute that dealt with intelligence problems, a huge information and computer complex, centers for cyphers and communications, special top secret laboratories, and places for preparing false documents. There were also big shops for the people who worked in the facility, and there was even a museum devoted to the history of the "knights of the cloak and dagger."

The First Chief Directorate continually grew, especially during the period when Yuri Andropov was in charge. Andropov loved intelligence, considering it to be the most important instrument of state policy, and supported the First Chief Directorate in every way. It was in his time that the directorate moved from the Lubyanka to Yasenevo and took over the tall, snow-white buildings. It was also during that time that the number of people employed in "residencies" abroad rapidly increased. An institute was founded; an effective analytic service was set up; and Andropov believed it necessary to spend a day or two of every week at the First Directorate. Because of this Andropov is still worshipped within the foreign intelligence service.

Lest my words about Andropov seem unfounded, I quote a recognized authority, William Colby, former director of the FBI. Colby once told a correspondent of the Russian magazine *New Times*, "In my view he was a very interesting person. He began by creating a new KGB, that replaced cutthroats previously working in intelligence. He took the best graduates from the country's best universities, taught them languages, and gave them good professional skills. And they really did work very well."

In Andropov's time, every morning dozens of unmarked coaches travelled the streets of Moscow to collect ordinary-looking men and women and transport them to Yasenevo—"to the forest" as the would-be spies called it. In the evening, when the working day was over, the same coaches returned the same people to their subway stations.

To go to work "in the forest" was the dream of every employee of the KGB. The intelligence service was always surrounded with an air of mystery and romance. It was considered the profession of the elite. More importantly, however, Yasenevo was thought to be a direct route to foreign countries, a secure life, and good money. Two or three lengthy foreign assignments and you could reckon to have secured yourself a comfortable old age. And, although the selection process was quite strict, it was by no means always the most worthy candidates that were taken into intelligence work. By hook or by crook, the children of the party *nomenklatura* and marshals and generals made it in. Personnel policy was seriously affected when people whose only qualifications were their previous work in CPSU committees were allowed into the intelligence service and equally importantly, placed in the more responsible jobs. It was thought that by doing this the CPSU was ensuring control over the state security organs and strengthening their ranks ideologically. I sometimes met such "party spies:" they were easy to identify because of their poor knowledge of foreign languages, their near-total lack of professional skills, and their great self-confidence. They didn't know how to do anything, but still, because of long-established habit, they looked down their noses at everyone else.

It was the First Chief Directorate that controlled my work at Radio Liberty. Although my first visit to "the forest" did not occur until after my return to Moscow, I had regular meetings with people from Yasenevo during my twenty years in the West. They would travel to the West to give me instructions or to pick up materials I had collected or prepared for the Center, and would come to Karlshorst to teach me special skills.

Within the First Chief Directorate, it was the so-called external counterintelligence—directorate "K"—that dealt directly with me. If I am not mistaken, that directorate was set up in 1971, based on the fourteenth department of the "second service" of the FCD, to stop the recruitment by other countries of Soviet citizens and, above all, to stop employees of the special services from working beyond the borders of the USSR, and to prevent enemy agents from penetrating the center of the intelligence service.

At the Lubyanka, counterintelligence functions were generally performed by the Second Chief Directorate, which still exists today (under a different name) in its old place in the center of Moscow. It is this agency that keeps foreigners under observation, controls the work of the legal *rezidentura* in Soviet embassies, and prevents both the establishment of spy networks on Russian territory and leaks of secret information. Counterintelligence means something different within the First Chief Directorate. There it is a sort of secret police within the secret service. One of its basic tasks, as I have already said, is to prevent the penetration of enemy agents into its ranks. Apart from that, the people working in directorate "K," known as security officers, take care of all Russian citizens who are working in official institutions or are on short assignments abroad.

In the old days the security officer in any Soviet embassy was all-powerful. Everyone was afraid of him: one bad reference from a security officer and a person would never go abroad again. Never.

I don't know what it's like in Langley, but our foreign counterintelligence always had plenty of work. Until very recently, the Soviet Union was a closed society, a country behind the "iron curtain." Because of this, it was very difficult for any foreign intelligence service to obtain access to secret information. The totalitarian regime knew how to keep its secrets safe. Practically any contact, however fleeting, between a Soviet citizen and a foreigner became known to counterintelligence.

Oleg Tumanov's father, Alexander Vasilevich Tumanov.

1945. Oleg Tumanov at eight months of age
with his aunt.

Tumanov in the summer of 1964 aboard the Soviet destroyer, *Spravedlivy*.

Munich 1967. The sweater Tumanov is wearing was a present from Yul Brynner's sister, Katya, who worked as a secretary at Radio Liberty.

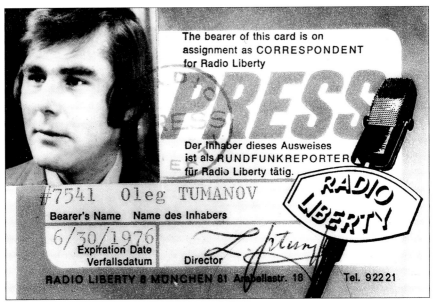

The bearer of this card is on assignment as CORRESPONDENT for Radio Liberty

PRESS

Der Inhaber dieses Ausweises ist als RUNDFUNKREPORTER für Radio Liberty tätig.

RADIO LIBERTY

#7541   Oleg TUMANOV

Bearer's Name   Name des Inhabers

6/30/1976
Expiration Date
Verfallsdatum   Director

RADIO LIBERTY 8 MÜNCHEN 81 Arabellastr. 18   Tel. 9 22 21

The perfect cover: a Radio Liberty press pass issued in 1971.

Tumanov arrives for a vacation in Las Palmas, Spain, in November 1973. In the canvas bag are secret documents that will be presented to the KGB a few days later in Moscow.

KGB Colonel Oleg Maximovich Nechiporenko, a KGB superior and friend of Tumanov's.

Tumanov with his wife, Yeta-Svetlana, in Munich, 1979.

Oleg and Yeta-Svetlana's daughter, Sasha, with the family dog, Krylat, in Munich, 1983.

Tumanov at a press conference in Moscow, April 28, 1986.

Reliving his twisted life story, Tumanov works on his book in Moscow, 1992.

In front of the KGB headquarters in Moscow, 1993.

Under such conditions, attempts to recruit people of interest to Western special services were, as a rule, doomed to failure.

At the same time, demands for information from the military-industrial complex, the field of science, top military circles, and, of course, higher levels of the party and state, were great. The West has always been afraid of the unpredictable "Russian bear" and wanted to know what its intentions were—at all times.

Beginning in the 1960s, to the great delight of the foreign special services, the Soviet Union began to allow a few of its citizens to travel abroad—groups of tourists, sports teams, official delegations, and others. These people became objects of close attention to foreign intelligence services, who began to look for weak spots. I do not wish to suggest that they recruited everyone at once: they preferred to catch only big fish. What could they get out of a soccer player or a housewife? But a well-informed journalist, an employee of a diplomatic mission, a nuclear scientist or an analyst, or, if you were lucky, even a KGB officer—these were sought-after catches for the CIA and other intelligence departments.

Soviet foreign intelligence services defended the interests of their country without meddling in the internal affairs of other countries— with some great successes. The results were especially striking in instances where they successfully introduced their people into those "objects" that were aimed directly against the USSR. Such objects undoubtedly included Radio Liberty.

I will now reveal, for the first time, a few episodes concerning this subject.

When I began to work for the First Directorate, the Center advised me to make a careful study of an Armenian named Diran Magrablyan. At the time, Magrablyan was in his trial period, working in Max Rallis's office, and was a candidate for a job in the special projects department. A so-called International Literary Association, with headquarters in Rome and offices scattered around the world, was organized under the aegis of this department. The formal task of the association was to develop cultural exchanges between the East and West. Although some of the Association's work may have been legitimate, it undertook other activities that were not. For instance, using money from the CIA, the association bought about a third of the books written in Russian, but published in other countries, and distributed them to Soviet citizens directly, or through the mail, for free. In the latter case, the chance of even one parcel out of a hundred reaching its addressee was almost nil: the censor at the Moscow international post office opened all correspondence from abroad. But even such slight chances were taken.

I became friendly with Diran, while always keeping my superiors informed of his activities—even when he moved to Paris, where he continued to "develop cultural exchanges." The Center occasionally asked me to approach Magrablyan to determine the channels through which the undesirable literature travelled. After one such request, I used a vacation to Paris with an Estonian named Raimo Randa as a cover for my investigation. Raimo and I set off for this vacation in his old Renault. In no hurry to get anywhere, we stopped frequently, saw the sights, and, in short, behaved like tourists. After three days, we arrived in Paris, where I stayed with Diran and his sister Sonya somewhere in Ivry, while Raimo stayed with a fellow Estonian.

The next day my hosts took me to the Paris office of Radio Liberty, where Sonya worked as a secretary. Linda Petrouskiene, a French citizen of Lithuanian origin, was the senior secretary at the station and was also a colleague of Max Rallis's. Max warned me that Linda maintained close contacts with American intelligence in Paris, and that she eagerly sought out, attempted to get to know, and sounded out Soviet citizens visiting Paris about their views on collaboration.

We went to lunch at a nearby bistro. On one side of me sat Diran, who for some reason preferred to remain silent, and on the other was Linda, who chattered on throughout the meal. She spoke in great detail about herself and her colleagues, occasionally asking my opinions of employees of the Munich office of Liberty. I replied conscientiously, trying not to go into great detail. Then, in the middle of a stream of absolutely harmless chatter, I heard, as if by chance, Linda ask:

"You say you attended courses at the Moscow Institute of International Relations . . . I have a friend there who sometimes comes to Paris. Perhaps he lectured to you sometime?"

"What is his name?" I inquired.

Linda named a man who had indeed given two or three lectures on international relations that I had attended. I remembered that he held a high position in the Soviet *nomenklatura*.

"Yes, there was such a man," I said calmly. But Linda seemed to have forgotten her question and turned the conversation to something else.

The subject of the lecturer never again arose in our talks. But there was something else. According to Linda, she often visited a small hotel where Soviet tourists and other visitors liked to stay—it was cheap.

"It's so funny," she said. "When they first come these people are afraid of their own shadow. They see CIA agents and provocateurs everywhere. But when they need to earn some money, they pull vodka, caviar, and wooden dolls out of their cases and are not in the least afraid to ask me to sell them. I am one of them. The possibility of obtaining foreign currency completely drives all the instructions they have been given in Moscow out of their minds."

I made a note of that conversation.

Meanwhile my stay in Paris was coming to an end. Through my talks with Diran I had learned how the illegal dispatch of books and brochures to the USSR was organized. It turned out that both the book association and the NTS were still making use of normal postal facilities. In Paris I saw lists of Soviet citizens, including their addresses in Moscow, Leningrad, Kiev, and Sochi. Parcels were sent to those addresses in accordance with instructions from the CIA (the action was given the name "Arrow"). Although, as I have already pointed out, there was practically no chance that the books would ever reach their destinations through these channels, the Americans did not hesitate to expose the people to whom they sent the books to reprisals from the KGB. After all, it was nearly 1970, and every kind of dissidence was being severely punished. Yet here was a man being sent a packet of anti-Soviet literature. Why precisely to that man? What contacts did he have with the special services in the West? What sort of character was he? The KGB put under observation every person to whom one of the parcels was addressed, although many of them suspected nothing and were quite loyal to the system. The lives of many Soviet citizens were destroyed for many years simply because they were the addressees for the parcels of books. Why didn't the organizers of Arrow think of this?

During my next meeting with the messenger from the Center I turned over all of the information I had gathered in Paris, asking that special attention be paid to the lecturer at the international institute—this is what came of that report.

As it turned out, the lecturer had risen in importance in the Soviet political system during my absence from Moscow. He had access to the most important party and state documents, was received by the most important people, and was head of one of the best-known social organizations.

Had Linda really hooked a big fish?

The story went like this. It appears that during an official assignment in Paris, the Americans had noticed the lecturer's passion for the Russian books sold in a special shop. Linda was carefully introduced to him as an assistant in the shop. She summoned up all her charms to please the guest from Moscow, and he promised that he would return to Paris.

It became clear in Moscow that, before taking any further steps to get closer to this man, the Americans would submit him to a careful background check. That is what happened. The CIA spent the next three years preparing a dossier on the "lecturer." At the same time, the KGB was not idle. With approval from the top party leadership (which was essential in such matters), and the cooperation of the lecturer, the KGB planned an operation they called "Apostle." I was assigned the role of observer and controller for this affair.

In 1973, our "Apostle" reappeared in Paris. One must give the American system its due: they knew exactly when people of operational interest to the special services departed for the West. The arrival of Apostle was immediately recorded and Linda Petrauskiene appeared on the scene again—almost instantly. Apostle was of course delighted to meet Linda again. He recalled that Linda had given him perfume for his wife on his last visit and complained about his poor health and the difficulty of getting treatment in the Soviet Union. These latter comments—about his illness and the difficulties in getting proper medical care—were absolutely true.

Linda's response was exactly as the KGB had hoped. She said she knew a lot of doctors in Paris, that their services were, of course, expensive, as were the medicines, but that there was nothing she wouldn't do for a real friend. They parted, quite pleased with each other.

Max Rallis attended their next meeting, introducing himself simply as a journalist interested in Soviet affairs. Apostle said he was quite ready to talk to any friend of Linda's, and by recounting rumors and anecdotes about the top people in the Kremlin, let it be known that he was well-informed. On that occasion he didn't reveal any great secrets, but hinted that he could tell us a great deal but did not have the right. That was enough for Rallis—the client was obviously ripe for real recruitment.

"Incidentally, we are very concerned about the state of your health," Rallis said to the visitor toward the end of the meeting. "Linda has told me something about it. Friends don't have the right to overlook this. We would like to help you get well."

Rallis then took out his wallet and handed Apostle a substantial sum in French francs.

"Take these, they will pay for a visit to the doctor and also help buy the medicine you need."

At first the visitor refused, but Max knew how to get his way.

"We will treat this money, not as a gift, but as a fee for the interview you have given me. After all, I can use what you have told me in my articles, can't I? Without mentioning the source, of course. Here in the West we pay well for such services."

Much later I read a detailed account of that meeting in the KGB archives.

I visited Paris again a month after Apostle's visit. Naturally I dropped by the office of Radio Liberty. Linda and Sonya were glad to see me. We chatted over coffee in a bistro and from their chatter I gathered that Linda had, for some unmentioned services, been promised that she would soon be promoted and receive a raise. I congratulated her sincerely; she fully deserved it.

There was then a long break in my Paris friend's contacts with Apostle, however. His illness had gotten much worse. He was not a young man, and he had to go through a serious operation followed by a long period of recuperaton. But espionage is just a matter of waiting. The winner is the one with the strongest nerves and the most patience.

American intelligence celebrated their "victory" in Belgium where the "recruitment" of the highly placed official from Moscow finally took place. It was carried out by two field agents of the CIA, introduced to Apostle as Michael Martin and Richard. In Michael's case the First Chief Directorate quickly established his real name—O. Selsky. Neither I, nor my colleagues, were ever able to learn anything about Richard, however.

It wasn't easy for Apostle to play the double game. He had, after all, not been through any special training, he was not young, and he had been spoiled by his high official position. Without any particular risk to his career Apostle could have told the KGB to get off his back—if not straight out, then with a specious excuse—the state of his health, for example. But Apostle decided conscientiously to take part in the intrigue. Although fifty-two years old, he agreed to go through an accelerated course of special training, including autogenous training and some work with a psychologist. The people in Moscow were afraid that the Americans would want to check Apostle with psychotropic drugs or submit him to a lie detector test. The KGB had its own lie detector and decided to acquaint Apostle with it in advance; at the same time, they decided to teach Apostle how to trick it. At that time Soviet intelligence was developing its own method for resisting the lie detector. They had progressed from the time when they instructed me to "drink a glass of vodka before the test and you'll have nothing to fear."

The Americans protected their agent very carefully. He was never contacted in Moscow, although there were ample opportunities to do so. They did not want to take any risks in this highly promising operation. All contacts, therefore, took place only on the territory of Western countries, mainly in France. Apostle regularly delivered highly confidential information—about the situation in the Politburo, the balance of forces in the Soviet leadership, and prospects for relations between the USSR and other countries—to American intelligence. He was interrogated in detail about the chances that Yuri Andropov would become the first man in the Soviet state. They inquired about what was behind the transfer of Andrei Gromyko from the position of foreign minister to head of the Presidium of the Supreme Soviet. How firmly placed were the leaders of the republican parties? What was the reason for Konstantin Chernenko's temporary absence from the political scene? What was going to happen at the next meeting of the Central Committee of the CPSU? What changes in leadership were to be expected in the near future? They asked him hundreds of similar questions.

Of course, on the eve of every meeting, the KGB provided Apostle with detailed instructions on how to reply to a variety of questions. Moscow wanted to keep the game going for as long as possible because the questions put to the double agent enabled them to assess how well the enemy was informed and to discover the channels through which information was being leaked. Apart from that, it was occasionally possible to feed the CIA specially fabricated disinformation through Apostle.

The Americans paid Apostle generously, both in rubles and in foreign currency. For reasons of security, he was advised to spend the francs only when abroad—to help him, they made a special container, which looked like the kind of mirror that one would carry in a bag of toiletries. The mirror separated into two pieces and the money was put between them. It was closed with a special substance that made it impossible for the secret hiding place to be detected by any device then known to Soviet customs. That mirror-container is now preserved in the KGB museum in the Lubyanka.

There were soon signs that the Americans were preparing to hold more frequent meetings with Apostle. They examined the house he had near Moscow, including approaches to it, and they studied the possibility of arranging hiding places. The operation, however, came to an unexpected and sad end, for both sides, when Apostle died suddenly in 1985.

I still don't know whether the Americans ever guessed that they were being led by the nose. If they did not know, then I offer them my sympathy in connection with what I have written.

Successes and Failures
of the Fifth Directorate

The case I have described demonstrates clearly the CIA's attempt to realize its Project Number 46, which was specially devised for Radio

Liberty and Radio Free Europe—more precisely, for the branch of the intelligence service operating under cover of the radio station. As I have already said, its main unit was the so-called Department for the Study of the Audience and the Effectiveness of Radio Broadcasting. At first this department was located in Munich but it was later moved to Paris. Today, as far as I know, it is part of the "Scientific Research Institute" attached to Radio Liberty/Radio Free Europe in Munich. The department was staffed by permanent employees of the American intelligence service and people closely connected with it. Their main task was to work with Soviet citizens temporarily stationed abroad: opinion surveys based on specially devised methods, the study of their questionnaires and, finally, if the "object" represented any intelligence value, his handling and recruitment. The department directed a vast network of informants who worked out of the Soviet embassies in practically all the countries of Western Europe. Their work had two main directions: One of them, Project 46, I have already mentioned; the other, Project 52, provided for similar work with people living permanently in the West.

On the basis of information received from the *rezidenturas*, Max Rallis's department prepared and distributed: information of an intelligence nature, as well as information about Russian citizens who had access to secret materials, to the CIA and military intelligence; information about the political and economic situation in the Soviet Union to the State Department; and information that could be used to prepare programs to the administrators of Radio Liberty/Radio Free Europe.

The fact that I write about these activities in the past tense by no means indicates that they are no longer going on in Munich. Of course, because of the changes that have taken place in our country, there have been some changes in how the secret work at Radio Liberty and Radio Free Europe is conducted, but the work itself has remained essentially the same. The intelligence service is reluctant to part with its familiar stereotypes. It seems probable that the Americans will continue to regard us as the crafty Russian bear that they have to watch closely for a long time. Incidentally, I don't think that our people have completely finished their work in the American direction either. Of course, it is not so easy for them now: the KGB is no longer supported by a superpower for which agents eagerly agree to work (for money or for the idea). There is no hard currency to pay for specific services, and there is no certainty about tomorrow. Traitors from among the officers in the legal *rezidenturas* reveal to counterintelligence services the agent networks in various countries. Many play a double game. It may well be that there has never been such a situation in the history of Russian espionage. But what can be done? Things are not going very well for any of us now. I am absolutely sure of one thing: that we do not have the right to completely abandon our intelligence efforts. The world is still far from perfect, and trust and honesty in dealings between states remain, for the time being, just an illusion. If I am wrong, why do the special services of other countries, using a variety of channels, continue to interest themselves so intently in our affairs? And why does Radio Liberty, with all its shady branches, still exist?

But I will return to the main subject of my narrative.

When I was working in Munich I had frequent occasion to be convinced of the great secrecy surrounding the work of Max Rallis's department. As was the rule, every "source" was allotted a code name or pseudonym, and the computers containing information about sources were fitted with reliable security systems. Only an extremely small circle of permanent employees of the CIA had access to such information.

If you think I am now going to start boasting about myself, that I managed to steal lists of secret agents abroad, you are mistaken. That nut was too hard for me to crack. The list found on George Perry's desk hardly counts—the people on it were small fries. Throughout my career I never attempted to break into a safe, to fit cyphers to other people's computers, or to poison anyone. I took no part in any shootings or quarrels, I did not change my appearance with false beards, and I never made a parachute jump. I was no James Bond. I was a typical spy of the end of the twentieth century. Painstaking information collection and analysis—that was what permitted me to achieve success from time to time.

I have already described how in 1967 I came together by chance with Eugene Parta, the American of Finnish origin who was later to become deputy to Max Rallis and who in 1981 took over Max's position as head of the department. Eugene never forgot the modest service I had done for him and through all those years kept up with me, maintaining warm, if not friendly, relations. Of course I tried not to let him out of my sight, which was easy, because he visited Munich regularly.

I must point out that the Center followed all of Parta's movements very closely. I believe that I was only one of a number of people the Center had watching Parta, for everywhere he appeared one had to expect surprises.

Our joint efforts established that Parta made frequent visits to Finland and that the final destination in each trip was Helsinki. At the same time the KGB noticed that from time to time, when Parta went to Paris, he was visited by a Finnish citizen and journalist, named Karl Kiuru. Further research revealed that Kiuru had a strong interest in the Soviet Union, or rather, in certain regions of Central Asia that were open to foreigners. It appeared that he had friends and acquaintances there. External counter-intelligence handed the material over to internal counterintelligence, the Fifth Directorate of the KGB.

It was not difficult for the Directorate to discover that among Karl Kiuru's Central Asian acquaintances was a young scientist who he always visited in the course of his trips to the USSR. They would meet and talk. The scientist did not divulge any special secrets, but he was very fond of arguing—talking and boasting—especially in the presence of foreigners. Intimidated by the attention being paid him by the KGB, the scientist immediately agreed to engage in a cat-and-mouse game with Kiuru. In the course of future meetings, the scientist would slip Kiuru some previously prepared information and observe how the Finn reacted to it.

Karl Kiuru took the bait. His visits to Central Asia became more frequent, and on each visit he brought gifts and took away phony material prepared by the KGB. The material given to Kiuru ended up in Eugene Parta's hands.

The game went on for quite a long time. (I suspect that the people in the Lubyanka couldn't figure out how to bring it to a satisfactorily end.) Kiuru was of course a straightforward spy and it was not especially difficult to catch him in the act. But that was exactly what the top people in the KGB did not want. For several decades, relations between Finland and the USSR had been marked by a special friendliness and trust. Our leaders would hardly have been pleased to have such a pitiful agent exposed—in major policy matters, that would have brought the Soviet Union no substantial benefit, and it could have cast a shadow over their relations with Finland.

In the end the operation was wound up very simply: during the course of a regular visit, Karl Kiuru was confronted by counterintelligence officers and politely asked for an interview. He was not presented with an arrest warrant or handcuffed, and he was not even asked to go along to the nearest police station. Karl was extremely scared and thought it best to tell them how Parta had recruited him, how the Americans financed his risky trips to the USSR, and about the instructions he had received from them. He was particularly concerned at the prospect of his story being published in Finland. The Finnish authorities would not have been pleased to learn that Karl Kiuru was a spy, or that, contrary to the laws of his country, he had been working for a foreign special service.

To get counterintelligence to take pity on him, Kiuru told all he knew about CIA activities in Finland that were directed toward the USSR.

After that he was released and told that he should never again appear in our country for such a purpose. He was also asked to tell Eugene Parta that the KGB considered the game over.

In my view, these operations can be regarded as manifest successes on the part of the Soviet state security or, more precisely, the Fifth, that is, the ideological directorate of the KGB. Apart from keeping an eye on the media, the intelligentsia and religious institutions, the Fifth Directorate was called upon, along with the First Directorate, to carry out actions to counter the ideological subversion organized from abroad, to oppose the émigré organizations and their contacts in the USSR, to coordinate efforts to jam radio broadcasts aimed at Soviet listeners, and to seize parcels of anti-Soviet literature and leaflets. There were similar counter-intelligence organizations throughout the Soviet Union and they, of course, also wanted to distinguish themselves in the campaign against enemy ideology and its adherents. With the permission of the bosses in the Lubyanka, they organized their own actions against foreign anti-Soviet centers—primarily the NTS, which was always considered to be the main enemy.

Surprises on the Way

I preferred East Berlin as the site for my rare meetings with colleagues from the Center. There I could at least feel as if I were at home for a time. I could relax and didn't have to be so careful. I could allow myself to become again the Moscow lad, Oleg Tumanov. It stands to reason that every visit to East Germany had associated risks, but the system the KGB worked out with East German state security always worked faultlessly. Everything was provided for down to the last detail.

Only once did I feel uncomfortable on my usual route. Having finished my business in Karlshorst, with the help of friends I successfully passed through the border and customs barriers at Schoenefeld Airport and was sitting in the plane due to fly to Copenhagen. As usual, my passport did not record my border crossing and the last name on my ticket was distorted beyond recognition.

Suddenly armed border troops burst unto the plane, which was already full of passengers. Two of the soldiers, armed with automatic guns, took up positions by the exit, while a plump woman in a mousy-colored uniform started checking everybody's passports and tickets.

What a surprise! I stayed in my seat, waiting calmly to see what happened. The mousy border woman was poised over me. I handed her my passport and ticket. She calmly examined the documents and returned them to me without a word. Within five minutes the check was completed, the soldiers left the plane, and we taxied for takeoff.

Even today I am unable to explain the strange behavior of those border troops.

If I don't count that instance, I can say that my regular contacts with the Center took place without any special excitement. The program was always the same: at a pre-arranged time I would fly to East Berlin, or, less often, to Austria or Switzerland, where I would meet the messenger assigned to take my fresh information to Moscow. The messenger would give me new instructions and I would return to Munich. Such meetings never took place in Munich or within the territory of East Germany. If any exceptionally difficult situations occurred during our meetings, it was our own fault. This is what happened on one occasion in Berlin when I fell, seriously strained my leg, and had to be hospitalized in East Berlin. I was in jeopardy of being recognized, but because I was on leave everything turned out all right.

On that occasion I was lucky. If I had not been on vacation, what would have happened? It would almost certainly have meant disaster if I had returned from East Berlin to the West with a leg in a cast put on in a Soviet military hospital. But it turned out all right in the end.

That kind of breakdown is usually the result of ignoring the rules of espionage. An illegal agent is absolutely forbidden to do many things that normal people do. You very seldom get away with breaking the rules. Here is another story on this subject.

On one occasion in Berlin I went fishing with my friend Sergei. Without knowing it, we ended up on the grounds of the country house of the head of East German security, Z. Milke. It was a specially protected zone that was strictly forbidden to enter. We were challenged by an East German guard. The situation was finally resolved peacefully and the Germans escorted us to our car, warned us severely not to do it again, and let us go.

Just imagine the fuss that could have arisen if the Germans had stuck to the rules and demanded my documents. An employee of Radio Liberty (linked directly with the CIA) had gone fishing under the very nose of the head of state security of the workers' and peasants' state. I couldn't have explained to them that I was a phony anti-Soviet person and that I was carrying out secret work for Moscow. That was why it was secret, so that no one would know about it.

Thank goodness that on this occasion it all ended without incident.

On another occasion my regular meeting was to take place in Austria. Bad weather intervened and the exchange nearly failed to take place. But it was all right in the end, thanks to an enterprising driver.

Incidentally, I never saw that driver again. He was a passing acquaintance, the kind who appear only once. Such people are very rare. Usually I would be introduced to a contact in Karlshorst, for example, and would then work with that person for a year or two. We were given minimal information about each other—just casual contact, harmless talk, quiet walks in the park. I had the final word on who I worked with: I could always reject a candidate for long-term communication work, which would cast doubt on his foreign assignment and his clandestine life in the West.

There was such a case in my experience.

On one occasion they produced the next candidate for work with me. He was older than I, extremely charming, by no means stupid, and at the outset didn't arouse any negative reaction. We got to know each other in the KGB apartment in Karlshorst. With her usual cordiality, Zoya laid the table and left the two of us alone. After a few drinks the new messenger suddenly became talkative. From what he said, I gathered that he had entered the intelligence service by way of the so-called party recruitment which meant that he had recently been a middle-rank party official somewhere in the depths of Russia, had been well thought of at that level, and as a reward, had been sent to the KGB school. After graduation, he had immediately been given the rank of major and now had been assigned to a job abroad.

According to my "legend" I was just the fugitive Sailor Tumanov who was collaborating with the intelligence service to earn my country's forgiveness. Consequently, according to his party standards, I stood a long way beneath him. So the fledgling "James Bond" started condescendingly giving me advice.

"Come on," he would say, "young man, make a really big effort and then our dear socialist state will perhaps receive you back again."

He talked at length about all kinds of "great successes and achievements of Communist construction" in which he had participated personally and in which I might possibly be involved in the future. I supplied him with vodka, listened, and nodded. When Sergei dropped in later in the evening I pulled my old friend aside and, without beating around the bush, asked him to excuse me from contact with this man.

Sergei looked at me inquiringly. "Why?"

I asked him over to the table. In a very short time he understood everything.

Each time I went to Karlshorst my instructors and I would always play a game. I would be asked if I could think of any KGB agents among my Radio Liberty colleagues. One time I was right on target. I named a Liberty editor who was indeed working for the organization. My friends asked why I was suspicious of the man.

"He always volunteers to work the night shift. Nobody wants to work at night, except (let's call him) Igor. I think he does it because he can roam freely, undisturbed, and rifle through offices, inspect desks and files, and photocopy anything he pleases," I replied.

My friends laughed. Igor was recalled shortly thereafter. When I returned to Russia, Igor and I met and had a couple of drinks. He now lives in St. Petersburg.

There were some curious episodes in connection with the arrival in Munich of guests from Moscow. One such episode took place in the course of the 1972 Olympic Games.

That summer I received a phone call from a friend, a former Soviet film producer who was working in the London office of Radio Liberty. When I was in England I nearly always stayed with him, and he used my apartment when he came to Munich. So I was not in the least surprised when he told me he would like to see the Olympics and asked to stay with me for a few days. On arriving, he let me know casually that here in Munich, traveling with a group of tourists from the Soviet Union, was a great friend from his school days whom he simply had to meet. Very well, but how did it concern me? I had a lot of work at the time and I did not attach any special importance to his words.

Then one day, on arriving home, I discovered to my great amazement that my London friend had invited his Moscow friend to my apartment.

It was unbelievable! Without warning a Soviet citizen had turned up as a guest of an employee of Radio Liberty! If the KGB got any hint of this it would be his end. He would be dragged through interrogations, all channels for promotion would be closed, and he would probably be dismissed from his job. He could forget ever travelling abroad again. His wife would leave him and at school the pupils would turn away from his children as if they had the plague. I remember how at the winter Olympics, a Radio Liberty sports commentator had exchanged a few words in passing at the press center with an old friend from Moscow, an ice-hockey writer with whom he had worked for many years. As a result the man from Moscow was dismissed from the newspaper and banned from being published in the central Soviet press. Yet their conversation had been completely harmless, an exchange of greetings, no more. Those few words were enough cause for the Fifth Directorate of the KGB to severely punish that journalist.

And now I had a guest from Moscow in my apartment! What's more, he was not in the least embarrassed. I immediately suspected that he was no ordinary tourist; more likely, he was a KGB officer or a so-called trusted person of the state security. He had apparently been included in the tourist group because of his childhood friendship with the émigré producer. They had instructed him to try to establish contact with people on the staff of Liberty.

It was a funny situation—would he really try to recruit me? He was certainly ready to try.

Would it be possible, he asked, to stay the night with me? It was late and the hotel was a long way away.

"Please do," I replied. "Spend the whole Olympics here if you like. So long as you won't have any problems."

"Oh, come on! What problems?" my guest lied brazenly. "Times have changed. There is a different attitude toward foreign travel in our country now. If I wish, I stay in a hotel, if not, I stay with friends. We must improve our mutual understanding, don't you think?"

"Of course, of course," I agreed eagerly and even shook hands warmly with him.

It was now quite clear what sort of character this man was. It was also clear that I must report that I had a man from the Lubyanka staying with me to my immediate superiors as quickly as possible. Early the next morning, while my friends were still asleep, I phoned Radio Liberty and told them about the daring Russian guest. A little later I had a call back: "Wouldn't your Russian guest like to meet someone from among the people in charge of Radio Liberty? Perhaps to breakfast together? Exchange impressions of the Olympics?" At seven o'clock in the morning, when their alarm went off and my friends awoke, and I passed on the invitation.

I was not surprised when the "tourist" agreed to the meetings without a moment's hesitation. I began to have doubts—perhaps he was not an intelligence officer but a dissident who had decided to ask for political asylum in the West?

We were met in a café not far from Radio Liberty, as I had expected, by Max Rallis's Munich deputy, my friend George Perry. But he was not alone. The director of Radio Liberty, Francis Ronalds, had expressed a desire to meet and talk with the Soviet visitor. Perhaps they too suspected that this was a man from the KGB, but had decided not to miss a chance to meet a fresh arrival from Moscow. Or, perhaps they expected him to request asylum in the West.

In such a situation it remained for me, a young employee of the radio station, to drink a cup of coffee and take my leave.

Our "tourist" did not ask for political asylum. Rather, he spoke very eloquently, said a lot about himself, and tried to provoke the others to speak frankly. He talked about the new progressive tendencies in the Soviet Union, about the general perception that even more progressive changes were on the way, and about the grandiose successes of Soviet society in every single sphere. He tried his best to be liked, going as far as to say that Radio Liberty's transmissions, according to him, played a tremendous part in the life of the Soviet people and were as popular as *Pravda*. (I can only imagine how pleased my superiors were to hear such flattery.)

"It's a great pity," our guest said, however, "that criticism of life in the Soviet Union takes up most of your broadcasts. You need to deal more with the positive processes taking place in our country. Devote more attention, not to politics, but to culture, sports, and music. Our young people are so fond of modern music!"

The "tourist" had so much to say that the breakfast developed into a lunch in a good restaurant, and on parting my bosses handed him some money and presents. As always, they didn't ask for a receipt but gave him the phone number of Radio Liberty.

I had practically forgotten about this strange fellow, when one day in Karlshorst Sergei asked, with an intriguing smile:

"Would you like me to amuse you?" and he handed me a typewritten account of the "tourist's" stay in Munich.

It was a curious document. Our guest (probably an employee of one of the republican branches of the KGB) had written detailed accounts of everyone he had anything to do with at Radio Liberty during the Munich Olympics. There was an exhaustive assessment of my friend from London, including a recommendation concerning his possible recruitment, and there were portraits of me, George Perry, and Francis Ronalds. About me, for example, he had the following to say: "If Tumanov is really the escaped sailor he makes himself out to be, he has had good training in the West. Cunning and clever, he is to be feared — he is a crafty enemy of the Soviet state."

I was delighted. Such a reference was for me the highest praise.

The "tourist" correctly ascertained George Perry's job. "This American of Polish (to judge by his accent) origin, is not really the journalist he claims to be. He obviously has other functions at Radio Liberty. He is probably an American intelligence officer. He has a weakness for women." Our director fared no better: "Francis Ronalds is an intelligent person who combines softness and decisiveness. But he knows absolutely nothing about Soviet affairs. You can spin him any kind of story and he will take it for the truth and sometimes use it in his work."

There you are—severe but quite objective judgments.

It may be that in Moscow the man received an award for such a successful penetration into the enemy's den. But, of course, this fleeting guest brought back nothing new. By then the KGB knew, if not everything, quite a lot about the main émigré organizations, including Radio Liberty. In the Lubyanka and at Yasenevo there were dossiers on every employee of the radio station. (These dossiers tell of strengths and weaknesses, and circles of acquaintances, and they note anything compromising, include analyses of writings, and tell of the subject's past.) Naturally, the secret police were not motivated by idle curiosity in doing this. The Politburo, as I have pointed out, regarded Radio Liberty as the most dangerous enemy in the conditions of bitter ideological confrontation. An enemy had to be studied, to have mines laid beneath him, and to be made weaker.

I suspect that at that time I was far from being the only man from the KGB in Munich and Frankfurt (where the headquarters of the NTS remained). There were instances when I would relate something that appeared to me to be very important to my bosses, only to have them add facts obtained from other sources. Sometimes colleagues would warn me about staff changes at Liberty and their forecasts were nearly always right.

In Moscow, preserved in steel safes in one of the KGB archives, I have seen bulging files with thousands of documents that deal with various aspects of Radio Liberty's work and staff. Some of the information, in fact quite a lot, came from me. The rest came from others—permanent employees of the intelligence service and agents recruited by them from émigré circles. Probably no one will ever know whether there are any like that now, or how many.

During my years of active service in the intelligence services, I never tried to recruit anyone. The Center categorically forbade any display of initiative. The people in Moscow wanted more than anything in the world to keep me in my job and to keep risks to a minimum. In my view, sometimes they were too cautious in this respect.

For example, when I suggested getting hold of some secret documents (I could simply have taken them, photographed them, and put them back), I was categorically forbidden to do so.

"You are too eager," they reasoned with me when we met. "You should arrange it so that the papers you want simply fall into your hands."

Easily said. Actually, really interesting documents did sometimes come my way, without any effort on my part. But as a young man I liked taking risks, walking on the razor's edge.

We had two secretaries working for us in the service—a Russian named Irina and a German named Gerda. They were both conscientious workers but, while Gerda coped well with the work, Irina would occasionally commit unforgivable errors. I once made successful use of one such mistake. One of the secretaries' duties was to distribute the mail—letters, newspapers, and internal correspondence. One day Irina handed me a paper signed by the president of Radio Liberty. I took it as I was leaving for home, dropped it in my case, and paying it no special attention, left. When I got home and began to read it I was dumbfounded. This secret document was only intended for the narrow circle of top people in Liberty—the director of the Russian service, the head of the research department, and two or three other leading officials. I was not, of course, included in that circle. It was my good fortune that Irina had mixed up the envelopes and given the document to me instead of Robert Tuck or Gerda von Deming (I don't remember which of them was then director). The document contained a very detailed analysis of the state of health of the general secretary of the Soviet Communist Party, Leonid Brezhnev, including the expected date of his death. It was immediately apparent that such information could only have been obtained from the people close to the Soviet leader or from his medical team. What is more, the document contained a forecast of the possible successors to Brezhnev: the names of Andropov and Chernenko were mentioned, but as far as Andropov's health was concerned the conclusion was very bad—he would not last long. Diagnoses were quoted and the possible progression of the disease was discussed.

Only the CIA could have been the author of such a document. On the top of it the president had written: "For your information, strictly confidential."

I immediately photographed the entire document and began to think about how I could send the material to my people. My regular meeting was not scheduled for a month. I had to make use of a special signal: I sent a letter, with a completely innocent text, to an agreed-on address in East Berlin. In it, by means of secret writing, I informed them that I had important information and asked them to arrange a meeting at once. Five days later a reply came from West Germany through the normal post. A coded message gave me the date and place of the emergency meeting. The material was dispatched successfully to Moscow. I heard later that they decided not to show it to the Central Committee of the CPSU—the

CIA's analysis of the prospects of the Soviet leaders was too gloomy.

But one has to give the Americans their due—all their prognoses came true.

The Murder of the Century

Mountains of books have been written about the tragic assassination of the American President John F. Kennedy. There are a number of theories on who shot the President, who was behind the assassin, and who covered up the assassin's tracks. Lee Harvey Oswald figures significantly in one way or another in all of these theories. It was our misfortune that shortly before the assassination Oswald returned from the Soviet Union where he had lived for a time and had even married a Russian girl. How could one pass over such a remarkable ground for accusing the KGB of having a part in the affair? It could not have been simpler: Oswald was recruited in Moscow, trained as a sharpshooter, a plan for the assassination was devised, and Oswald was sent back to the States. Even now there are many Americans who believe that.

The version that included the participation of the Kremlin in the "murder of the century" grew in popularity when it became known that there really had been contacts between Oswald and the KGB. In the West, Colonel Nechiporenko's name has emerged in connection with the assassination.

Remember the dandy who chatted with me in the Sovietskaya Hotel in Moscow in 1965? I promised to go into more detail about him and the time has now come for that. Nechiporenko is remembered in the West not only in connection with the assassination of Kennedy. John Barron, the author of the well-known book on the KGB, tells of Nechiporenko's "Mexican period," describing him as the most brilliant officer of Soviet intelligence in Mexico. In his articles exposing KGB operations, General Oleg Kalugin accused Nechiporenko of having interrogated American airmen taken prisoner in Vietnam. I will reveal yet another secret connected with his name: He was the person who cared for Ramon Mercader, the man who murdered Lev Trotsky, when he was in Moscow after having served his sentence in a Mexican prison.

At the beginning of the 1980s fate again brought me in touch with Oleg Nechiporenko. But first I will go back seventeen years.

It was a Sunday in the autumn of 1963, on Calsad Takubay Street, number 204, in Mexico. Employees of the *rezidentura* of KGB foreign intelligence had organized a volleyball tournament on the embassy grounds. At the very height of the competition the duty officer summoned the deputy cultural attache, Nikolai Leonov, who was in fact a KGB officer, from the court.

"Some strange character has turned up here. Says he's an American. Wants an urgent meeting with someone from the embassy. A very strange type . . . "

Just as he was—in shorts and a T-shirt—Leonov received the American in the special room used for such unexpected visitors. Lee Harvey Oswald surprised him by his excited appearance. He gave the impression of someone who had just been through a deadly dangerous experience. Restless eyes, excited movements, sweaty hands, and confused speech—it was not surprising that the duty officer had been alarmed. To cap it off, after having sat down in the chair offered him, Oswald pulled an impressive revolver of a very large caliber from his belt and placed it on the table in front of him. Nikolai Leonov noticed that the gun was fully loaded.

"They are following me," the American explained. "They are literally breathing down my neck. Any moment they can kill me."

"Calm down—there's nothing to threaten you here. Tell me exactly who you are talking about."

"Agents of the American special services—who else!" the visitor replied aggressively. "They follow on my heels. They are everywhere. But I won't be an easy prey. They will pay dearly." With that, Oswald grabbed the gun and started waving it in the air.

Leonov had great difficulty calming down the unusual visitor and dragging out a few coherent sentences. From their discussion, it emerged that Lee Harvey Oswald had lived in the Soviet Union, had worked in a factory in Minsk, and had then returned with his Russian wife to the United States. He was now seeking refuge from the American special services, who he said were following him.

"So what brings you to us?" Leonov asked Oswald.

"I want to return to the USSR. That will be my salvation. Give me a visa. Right now, no dithering."

"But that's impossible. You must write an application which will then be studied in the proper way and the appropriate decision will be made. You understand, I hope, that I can't decide that matter on my own."

"But I can't wait!" Oswald again broke into a shout. "They want to kill me today, they're in my hotel. They have recruited the woman who cleans my room, but I'll do away with her first."

At this point Leonov, as he told me afterwards, became very frightened. After all, if this madman really did kill somebody the investigation would inevitably reveal that he had visited the Soviet embassy. The two things would be linked. He made a great effort to calm Oswald and to dissuade him from any precipitous acts.

"Come and see us on Monday. I am sure that we will be able to do something to help you."

Finally, when Oswald was able to somewhat control his ardor he said, disappointedly: "Well, if you don't want to help your friend I will go to the Cubans. Maybe they will be more helpful."

During the next week, Oswald turned up at the Soviet embassy two more times. A man from the consular department talked to him on those occasions. He was Oleg Nechiporenko, a foreign counterintelligence officer. After that Oswald disappeared. And a short time later the shots in Dallas were heard around the world.

Oleg Nechiporenko told me that his talks with Oswald were similar in tone to the first talk Oswald had with Leonov. But he asked me not to reveal any details: Nechiporenko is writing a book about Oswald and promises to tell a lot of interesting things in it.

Incidentally, Nikolai Leonov later became head of the directorate of intelligence information of the First Chief Directorate, ending his career as a lieutenant-general and deputy to the chairman of the KGB. He knows a lot of intriguing secrets about foreign intelligence. The details about the first meeting with Lee Harvey Oswald reported here have never been published before—I am revealing them for the first time.

As for Nechiporenko, he continued to work under the cover of the consular department for another year and a half and then returned to Moscow. It was at that time that our meeting took place in the Sovietskaya Hotel, on the eve of my "escape" from the warship. Later Nechiporenko had another long assignment in Mexico. He had a brilliant knowledge of Spanish, was young, energetic, and full of ambitions. Spying came naturally to him. Nechiporenko once said to me: "Recruiting an agent gives me pleasure comparable with what a woman you love can give you in bed."

He worked in external counterintelligence against the Americans. In his book about the KGB, John Barron devotes quite a few pages to Oleg Nechiporenko. Barron says that Nechiporenko's command of Spanish enabled him to speak the slang of the peasants, the truck driver, and the student, but when necessary, he could switch into the faultless language of diplomats and grandees. Barron supposed that he was half Spanish, but that is not true. Nechiporenko was born in Moscow and graduated from the institute of foreign languages. His brother Gleb also served in foreign intelligence, where he dealt with "illegals." He was a competent artist and engraver and for a long time played a part in the manufacture of false documents. Later he drew up routes and legends for illegals, and subsequently switched to operational work. In "the forest" he shared an office with Oleg Gordievsky who, as it later became known, worked for many years for British intelligence.

Oleg Maximovich Nechiporenko had some great successes during the eight years he spent in Mexico. Barron's many words of praise of Nechiporenko's great professionalism were well deserved, as I subsequently learned. Nechiporenko was probably the best KGB field operative in Latin America. More than once, the Americans approached him with tempting proposals to change sides. But he would only laugh and continue his game. It reached the point where on one occasion Nechiporenko penetrated into the most secret rooms in the United States embassy and wandered around calmly on the pretext that he was a member of an official delegation from Washington. The enemy's counterintelligence drew their own conclusions from this; in March 1971, taking advantage of the defection from the Soviet embassy of a technical employee, Raisa Kiselnikova, and her "revelations" (what could a mere typist know?), the Mexicans expelled five Soviet diplomats, including Nechiporenko, from their country. This move was accompanied by a noisy campaign in the press about an alleged KGB plot to organize a widespread partisan movement in Central America.

Nechiporenko's service did not end with his expulsion from Mexico. In directorate "K" he headed a department that dealt with international terrorism and ideological subversion. He acted as a consultant to the special services in Nicaragua and, using false documents, he had secret meetings with KGB people in other countries. He was twice in Vietnam, which provided the basis for rumors that he interrogated American prisoners of war.

"In 1973 I did in fact meet one American prisoner," Oleg Maximovich told me, "but the meeting didn't go beyond general conversation. The Vietnam intelligence officers didn't let us get too close to the Americans and jealously watched our every move in that direction. A year later I spent some time in Hanoi again, but this time I was only allowed to see records of the questioning of prisoners. Incidentally, I must say that, to judge by that material, the Americans conducted themselves very correctly as prisoners. None tried to bargain for his life by means of treachery."

Like many others, Nechiporenko ended his career in intelligence in the First Chief Directorate's training school, the so-called Red Banner Institute. He headed the faculty that taught the art of spying. When he departed, that faculty was closed down. Does this mean that there are few people in the spy business who elevate their trade to the level of an art? For the majority it is, alas, the same kind of humdrum profession as that of librarian or accountant. I have never come across another so romantic practitioner of espionage as Oleg Nechiporenko.

The straw that broke Nechiporenko's back, and caused him to retire, was a decision by KGB head, Vladimir Kryuchkov, to have the entire staff of the central apparatus of the KGB, including counterintelligence, march in the traditional demonstration on the anniversary of the October Revolution on November 7, 1990.

"That was a display of sheer madness," Nechiporenko said. "People who had even concealed from each other that they worked for the special services were now obliged to show themselves to the people of Moscow, under the keen eyes of the television cameras in Red Square. The KGB column was followed by students from the Red Banner Institute—future officers of external intelligence who were training for distant assignments under the cover of being diplomats, businessmen, people working in foreign trade companies, or journalists. Only a madman would permit such a thing."

When Oleg Nechiporenko appeared in Austria for a meeting with me I was very surprised. He had a forged passport, in a different name, but had not bothered to change his appearance. By then, John Barron's book, which included his photograph and a description of his successes in Mexico, had been published. But he only laughed at my concern:

"Don't overestimate the resources of the Austrian counterintelligence. I am not of the slightest interest to them. The well-known terrorist, Ilich Carlos, travelled freely around the world with a false passport, scarcely bothering to change his appearance. He simply had himself photographed for the documents with very slight alterations: each time he moved the lighting or altered the camera angle."

"You mean to say you met with that murderer?"

"He passed through the USSR on several occasions," Nechiporenko replied without batting an eyelid. "We knew about it, but Andropov categorically forbade any contact with Carlos. He was afraid that eventually it would become known and there would be a great fuss."

I was grateful to Oleg Maximovich Nechiporenko, for it was he who had insisted that my relatives be told the truth about me. My father had by then already died without ever knowing what I was involved in abroad. That grieved me. I realized that my mother also did not have long to live. Did she really have to die with this heavy burden on her heart? Her son a traitor, a deserter who had abandoned his parents forever. I could imagine how hard it had been for her to continually think about that. The people in Moscow had guessed my mood, which is why they had assigned such an experienced officer as Nechiporenko to work with me. Much later he confirmed that was the case.

"Yes," he admitted to me, "we felt that you needed urgent psychological help. What were the signs? Well, it's difficult to explain. I suppose one would have to point to a combination of scarcely detectable changes in your behavior and to your latest reports to the Center. On the surface everything remained the same and nobody had the slightest grounds for having doubts about you, but to understand that you have to work in intelligence all your life.

"You were tired. At times you were not vigilant enough. You were taking excessive risks chasing after valuable information. It was quite explicable after having worked so many years without any accidents! Any person in your place would have had his sense of danger blunted."

Nechiporenko continued: "I approached the top people with radical suggestions for providing you with powerful psychological support. My suggestions were approved, the unusual idea of telling your family the truth about you. Normally we never do that, but in this case, after weighing all the pros and cons, the chiefs gave their permission. I met with your elder brother and we went together to see your mother. She was reduced to tears by the news that we brought her. After that I left for Austria."

Yes, I remember very well that meeting with Colonel Nechiporenko. He brought me a letter from my brother—the first he had written without the KGB censor looking over his shoulder—a real, moving letter from someone close. He told me about my mother. Nechiporenko was also the first person to give me an intelligible explanation of why the Center attached so much value to my work at Radio Liberty.

"Your information, Oleg, goes straight to the members of the Politburo," the colonel said. "Some of the most important party and state decisions on counteracting hostile propaganda and ideological subversion are made on the basis of your reports. Thanks to you we know about all the plans of our dangerous enemy and can inflict preemptive blows."

We were sitting at a corner table in a little restaurant that was crammed with tourists, noisy and smoky. Nobody paid us the least attention. It seemed as though the visitor from Moscow was pinning war medals on my chest.

"With the aid of your information we have compromised several CIA men who were working against our country, and we have prevented a series of major long-term subversive operations. The leaders of the counterintelligence service of the KGB asked me to convey their gratitude to you."

We raised our glasses and drank, first without clinking glasses together, then to my late father, then to our meeting.

After that the colonel set about carrying out the second, more difficult part of his task. His purpose was to give me some real training, without wounding my pride. He mainly stressed the need for caution and circumspection. He begged me not to display too much initiative, to consult more often with the center, and not to get carried away. I, of course, promised to follow his advice.

Nechiporenko was not, apparently, exaggerating when he said my work was valued in Moscow. An opportunity to again convince myself presented itself shortly thereafter. My next meeting was to take place in Karlshorst. Everything there was just as it had been during the ten years before: the friendly and very hospitable Zoya had prepared a good supper and my old friend Sergei had flown in from Moscow. I noticed, however, that the table had been laid differently, as if for a celebration. Expensive drinks — whisky, gin, and good French wine — had appeared from somewhere. And the snacks were obviously not produced locally but had probably been bought in the West. I looked inquiringly at Sergei:

"What's all this for? You have guests?"

"Yes," he said. "One of our big shots wants to have supper with you. He has heard about your achievements and decided to get to know you better."

Although small of stature, the guest really did turn out to be an important figure. (Later he held a very high position in the KGB.) He behaved like a typical big shot — he wasn't particularly interested in the details of my work, instead, he concentrated on the caviar and whiskey.

"We are pleased with your work," he said, chewing vigorously as he spoke. "Many of your reports are lying on the desk of Leonid Ilyich Brezhnev. There can be no higher praise for an intelligence officer — I hope you understand that?"

I nodded and muttered something like an expression of gratitude.

"But how do you feel? Perhaps you would like to express some requests or desires?"

"Yes, I would," I relied rather cheekily. "I made a request long ago that cannot be satisfied here."

Sitting in the next chair, Sergei was fidgeting nervously and trying to step on my foot under the table. I moved further away from him. I realized that I was breaking some unshakable bureaucratic rules, but I decided to carry on regardless. The big shot from Moscow stopped devouring caviar and stared at me with a certain alarm.

"I have asked several times that a trip to Moscow be arranged for me, but the problem just cannot be decided. Please understand that I have not been home for fifteen years."

The man from Moscow continued his interrupted meal with obvious relief. Perhaps he had thought I was going to ask him for a million dollars?

"So what about it?" he asked and turned to Sergei. "Is it really such a difficult problem to solve? Planes fly to Moscow every day. Buy up all the first-class seats. Arrange to go aboard before all the other passengers enter the plane. Well, in a word, I don't see any great problems here. This man is doing important work. Taking risks. We must help him."

"Very well, comrade General!" that was all Sergei said.

So at last I found myself in Moscow having caused my colleagues in counterintelligence a fair amount of trouble, since they had to arrange the trip. I was transported in a car with closed blinds. For the purpose of disguise, I was advised to let my beard grow and to always wear dark glasses. They put a Russian fur hat on my head, something I had never worn before. I took part in this masquerade readily because I realized how necessary it was. Nothing could spoil my state of elation: I was in Moscow, I was home!

First they arranged a meeting with my brother Igor. Then, late in the evening, Igor and my KGB escort drove me to see my mother. She knew nothing about my arrival in Moscow. My brother unlocked the door of the apartment where I had passed my childhood and led me into the room. My mother, who was then in the kitchen, followed us into the living room. When she saw Igor she was not surprised. But then, saying nothing, I stepped out from behind his back. A plate fell from her hands and broke into small pieces. She burst into tears.

She had aged considerably. She was sorry for me. She told me what happened to my childhood friends and what they were now doing. In her eyes I was a person for whom, because of the strange assignment that had taken me away for so long, everything had gone wrong. My life had not been a success.

"What a fate you chose for yourself!" was all she could say in sympathy.

The next day I visited my father's grave.

I made only two such brief trips "on leave" to Moscow in the course of twenty years! The trips would start during a vacation to Greece, for example. I would then travel from Athens to Copenhagen or Berlin and from there to Moscow, always being careful to change my name a little bit. (The CIA uses the same technique.)

Life in the West

The rich have funny ways. I will not say that in the West I made a great fortune, but I did live quite well without depriving myself of anything. Without noticing it, I acquired the habits of a typical well-to-do person. If I wanted to add to or renew my wardrobe, I invariably went to England, where clothes were expensive but the most fashionable in Europe. I not only bought things in the most respectable shops, but I also enjoyed shopping there and feeling that I was one of the regulars.

On one of these trips I stayed with my friend Vladik Davidenko. He was a very colorful character. In planning his escape from the Soviet Union, Vladik found himself a job as a stevedore in the port of Leningrad. For a long time he carefully studied how the border and customs systems worked and got to know their weak spots. Finally, after having carefully calculated the best moment, he boarded a ship leaving for Liverpool, hid in its hold and sailed to the shores of foggy Albion without being noticed. For several days he was without food or water, but he had reached the object of his illegal journey—England. Mixing with a crowd of local stevedores, he left the ship without trouble.

When Vladik Davidenko stepped on English soil, his first desire was to satisfy his hunger. For this he went into the first café he came across, using hand gestures to indicate that he wanted. Naturally, they brought him everything he asked for. And he ate. When presented with the bill, Vladik firmly pushed it aside and asked that the police be called. When they arrived he declared:

"I, Vladislav Davidenko, have just arrived secretly in Great Britain, on orders from the Ukrainian National Front, for a meeting with the writer Anatoli Kuznetsov. I have brought him an extremely important message."

The British authorities believed the manifest rubbish and took Davidenko to meet Kuznetsov. Facing the rather worried writer, who lived in constant fear of revenge by the KGB, Vladik Davidenko made a clean breast of it, admitted that he had no message but wanted desperately to remain in the West.

Vladik began his new life working as a car mechanic. Later, as many others had done, he opened a Russian restaurant, called "Rasputin," and, like the majority of his predecessors, soon went bankrupt. To avoid his creditors, Davidenko fled to Munich and he tried to get a job as a manual worker at Radio Liberty. It was then that we became friends. Later Vladik Davidenko returned to London and went into the business of illegal trading in motor cars. His adventurous nature thirsted for such affairs Of course, the police pretty soon caught on to my friend; he ran away but was finally arrested and spent some time in prison.

When I visited him this time, Vladik had started a new business — a wine bar — and was again trying to get rich quickly through some rather questionable operations. In a word, he was in his element.

Vladik seemed genuinely pleased at my arrival. He invited a couple of his girlfriends and we set off to amuse ourselves, first in a restaurant and then in a Playboy Club. Some years before, one of the girls — Yeta — had emigrated from the Soviet Union to Israel. To avoid compulsory military service, she had later moved to Great Britain. When we met, Yeta was living hand-to-mouth. She worked as a secretary for the BBC, and on that basis has been given a certificate by the police that allowed her a temporary stay in Britain. She lived in a tiny one-room apartment.

I had just broken up with my latest Munich girlfriend and was wondering whether it was time to get married. I was tired of the disorganized life of a bachelor, and yearned for more stable domestic comfort. What's more, I was tired of the sidelong glances of colleagues that said: strange that Tumanov is not married. Perhaps he's homosexual? The real reason that I had not married was that all the potential wives (or their parents) I had come into contact with were connected in one way or another to Radio Liberty. To work for the radio station and then to be always getting involved in conversations about one's work at home and discussing the "destiny of the Russian emigration" was too much for me. In this respect, Yeta seemed far more attractive. True, she was a very frivolous person, but at the same time absolutely nonpolitical and not connected in any way with Liberty.

So the die was cast. It remained to get the consent, not of Yeta (I had no doubts about that), but of the Center. I was not at all sure that Moscow would approve of the marriage. I had to choose whether to risk taking this serious step and getting married without the knowledge of my superiors or to throw caution to the winds and go on living in the old way. I chose the first. In spring 1978, Yeta and I were married in a registry office in London. Our marriage lasted seven years.

To my surprise the Center reacted quite calmly, if a little coolly, to the event. Only Sergei, at our rare encounters, never failed to ask: "Hello — not divorced yet? And I've found you a wonderful wife in Moscow! Still young, but she will be just right for you when you come back home."

The first two or three years of married life went very smoothly. With the help of Alex and American counterintelligence, Yeta-Svetlana obtained a quite respectable German passport, known as a Fremdenpass. She completed a German-language course at the Goethe Institute in Munich and, unlike me, was able to write and speak the language quite well. She had known Hebrew from childhood and had a good command of English. With such qualifications it was natural that she didn't want to sit at home.

"I've found myself a job as a teacher of Russian at the U.S. Army's Russian institute," she announced one day. "I've already phoned Garmisch and they've invited me for an interview."

To say that I was upset is an understatement. It was the beginning of the first difficulties in my marriage. To hell with her desire to take a job at all costs. But in Garmisch of all places! Every one knew that, apart from the open institute, this was a secret establishment that belonged to and was co-located with American military intelligence. It was tempting to have one's own person there—that would promise unexpected successes in my secret activity—but how would the Center regard such a turn of events? Was it not a fatal mistake that might turn out to be my downfall? American counterintelligence would now become interested in my wife and would do a complete check on her before she was taken on to the institute staff. That meant they would be checking on me again. I had nothing particular to fear, but all the same.

My attempts to dissuade Yeta from her plan were to no avail. I couldn't tell her that I was a Soviet spy. Well, I could have with the Center's permission, but that would automatically have made Yeta my accomplice with all the consequences that would follow.

"Garmisch is a long way from here," I told her. "You will have to travel over sixty kilometers a day."

"But you know what a good driver I am," she replied.

"And they are not offering you very much money—just two thousand Marks. Is it worth the effort?"

"But it's for just two lessons a day."

A few days later I was summoned to the security department of Radio Liberty and asked what I thought about my wife being invited to teach in the Russian institute of the U.S. Army. I shrugged my shoulders as if to say it was all the same to me as long as it didn't have a bad effect on my work. (I was already the head of the news department.) To my amazement, the man I talked to begged me not to put any roadblocks in Yeta's way.

"You are very well thought of here," he explained. "You have been through all the necessary screening so there shouldn't be any special problems with clearing your wife. If she passes the exams successfully and joins the staff as a teacher it will be to the advantage of the radio station. The wives of our employees must work in prestigious places."

Once Yeta became a language teacher and interpreter in Garmisch, I had the opportunity to meet some of her pupils. They were not simple soldiers learning to speak Russian. After a little vodka, they were happy to explain that they would soon depart for Russia, with a new name and passport. I passed this information on to Moscow.

Yeta taught in Garmisch until 1982, when our daughter Sasha was born. She then found a job nearer to home.

An episode that I still can't explain occurred during one of my daughter's first crawls around our apartment. One day, when she was about one year old, Sasha crawled out of our bedroom with a strange object in her mouth. I took her by the hand and she spat out the object. It turned out to be a miniature microphone with a magnetic sucker that had been skillfully camouflaged as a screw. How had Sasha managed to detach the "bug," who had put it there, and when? I was seriously worried by this accidental discovery. What was it? A routine check that all employees were subjected to from time to time? Or had the counter-intelligence service turned on me in earnest?

I didn't think about the matter for very long, deciding that the best thing was to throw my find into the garbage. At the regular meeting in Karlshorst, however, I told my colleagues about the "bug," which apparently caused them much concern. They advised me to inspect the whole apartment carefully, paying attention to certain places, and to observe the rules of conspiracy more strictly. Back in Munich I carefully went around all the rooms, examining the walls and the furniture. I found nothing else suspicious.

It was no secret to anybody at Radio Liberty that employees of the security service entered their apartments to carry out secret searches when they were out. For that reason, I never kept any special equipment at home—apart from a container for photographic film made in the shape of an electric battery. The battery actually did power my radio receiver, but it also had a container inside.

One day, in the mid-1970s, I went to work leaving my new girlfriend in the apartment. Shortly after noon she phoned me—furious.

"Tell me, Oleg, who did you give the keys to the apartment to?"

"I didn't give them to anyone."

"Then I just can't understand it."

"Calm down and tell me what happened."

"I woke up because somebody was opening the door with a key. Thinking it was you returning from work I ran, half naked, out into the hallway. And there, for God's sake, stood two strange men. They said hello to me, turned around, and left. Tell me who they were?"

"Tell me what they looked like."

After she described the uninvited guests I had no doubt that one was the head of the Radio Liberty security service and the other was one of his colleagues.

Strangely enough, the affair of the "bug" was never followed up and remains a mystery to me.

I will return to my family life. During the Garmisch period I noticed that Yeta had acquired a number of new friends. She started returning late from work and was obviously lying when I questioned her. I didn't actually attach any special importance to this: I had enough worries— my appointment as head of the news department took up an enormous amount of time and energy. If for some reason Yeta did not return from Garmisch to sleep in Munich I was even glad to have the opportunity to be alone. I usually came home late from work, left for the office early in the morning, and was frequently called by phone during the night. In those days the news department was working around the clock and I had a very heavy workload.

I thought that everything would fall into place when our child was born—Yeta would leave Garmisch and devote herself entirely to the family. But that was not the case. My wife had hardly stopped breast-feeding Sasha when she found a new job, this time closer to home, in a special institute that belonged to the American military intelligence, located on the U.S. base in Munich. She found a nanny for Sasha and started again to surround herself with admirers.

It could not go on like that for long. We started to live apart and then I filed for a divorce. I received the documents dissolving the marriage after my return to Moscow.

In 1987, I began to live with another girlfriend. Her son Volodya was in school. I planned this book when we decided to marry.

Part III

Return to Moscow

Traitors

Traitors are the scourge of every intelligence service. They are the cause of the majority of failures by agents, cause panic in the Center, can upset whole governments, and their treachery can serve as grounds for major international scandals. By traitors, I primarily mean officers of the central intelligence organization who have access to information about the spy network.

Oleg Gordievsky, who defected to the British in 1985—after having worked for them for thirteen years—exposed many valuable sources in Europe and in South America. The treachery of officers of the legal *rezidentura* in Italy and France led to the collapse of Soviet intelligence networks that had specialized in obtaining scientific and technical secrets.

I was exposed by an officer of our external counterintelligence service, named Gundarev, who defected from Greece. He knew that the KGB had its own man in Radio Liberty and was able to list a number of indirect signs that pointed to me. In fact, he knew a great deal. When he defected, my superiors in Moscow became very worried, decided that my song was over, and that it was time for me to go home.

The Soviet Union celebrates its army and navy on a special day at the end of February each year. We also celebrated that day in Munich: anybody, like me, who had any connections to the Soviet armed forces, or had served in the Vlasov army, or even in the White Guards joined in the celebration. If you had seen military service you were expected to celebrate. On that day we would get together in good masculine company and drink plenty.

February 23, 1986, was no exception. On that Sunday, I returned home quite late after a friendly party, poured myself half a glass of vodka, drank it down with a crust of bread and a pickle, and began to warmly remember my far-away relatives in Moscow who had served in the Soviet military.

Monday was always my day off, so I was in no hurry to go to bed. The previous week had been difficult—I had worn myself out at work, so I decided to sleep late the next day. I had ordered a dozen of my favorite shrimp pastries, and different kinds of meat with sharp spices from the Chinese restaurant next to Arabella house. (I was particularly fond of those spring rolls.)

The telephone awoke me at six o'clock the next morning; not especially surprised, I picked up the receiver. A phone call at such an untimely hour was not rare—it meant that the night shift had encountered some problem and wanted to shift responsibility to me. It was quite possible that it was a trifling matter, but everybody liked to play it safe—I would phone the head of the department, inform him of what I had been told, and tell him I knew no more. It was rare for them to pass on something that was really important or that demanded my immediate attention.

So I picked up the receiver as usual, switched on the lamp, and prepared to listen to a complaining voice—"What are we to do, we can't find the tape that ought to have gone out already?" Somewhere at the other end of the line something clicked and squeaked and a cheerful Russian voice burst into my ear:

"Are you asleep, editor? Have you heard the latest news?"

I thought, gloomily, it seems as though someone has taken one drop too many. I'll get rid of him.

"Listen," the cheerful voice continued. "Tanya has given birth—a fine boy, weighs two kilos. They are all expecting you at the christening. Get rid of your American friends and come. They are all waiting for you."

What a cheerful, jolly voice!

Then it hit me like an electric shock.

"All right, I'll be there," I replied and put down the receiver, which now seemed like it was burning my hand.

It was the agreed signal for an alarm. "Tanya has had a boy." When I heard that sentence I was to wind up all my affairs at once and run without looking back. I was to run, using any of the channels worked out for such occasions, without asking the Center any questions or trying to get in touch with them, and without losing any time.

Something had happened. I was in serious danger. It was possible that I was already under observation by counterintelligence. It was possible that they would try to arrest me in the morning. The phrase "Tanya has had a boy" cancelled my settled, familiar life and demanded that I act quickly and decisively. This "birth" marked the end of my twenty-year career in Munich. Yes, I had to hurry.

Still in bed, I lit a cigarette and tried to work out a plan. It was still dark outside, but I knew that the taxis beneath my balcony were already waiting for passengers to go to the railroad station, the airports, wherever they wanted. You simply had to pay. But I quickly disposed of the wish to get straight into a taxi and get far away. No, I mustn't act like that. I had to make myself get up as usual, calmly wash and dress, grab some food from the Chinese, and take a walk—in a word, to behave as if nothing had happened. That would be my salvation. If I was being followed I must not appear to be alarmed in any way. Let them think I know nothing.

There was nothing compromising in my apartment—not a thing. A Nikon camera such as any well-off gentleman might have; a notebook that only contained the addresses and telephone numbers of legitimate friends and acquaintances; a cypher pad that on the surface looked like an ordinary notebook—but I set it on fire, just in case. I had no special radio, no weapons, and no poison pills (the kind that, according to fiction writers, a spy swallows if he is threatened with arrest). Nothing.

But there were other things—possessions that I had acquired over my years in Munich which were valuable both in the literal and personal sense: early eighteenth-century Russian engravings; paintings by the talented artists of the Soviet underground Oscar Rybin, Mikhail Shemyakin, and Oleg Tselkov; a nineteenth-century icon, Palekh work of the most delicate kind. I also had a unique library—the whole "White" archive and the rarest, volumes from the "Red" archive; periodicals of the Russian emigration in the 1920s and 1930s collected with great care over a long period; works by Russian philosophers; a complete set of the Vlasov movement's newspapers; a collection of the magazines *Granil, Posev, Kontinent, Syntaksis, Vremya i my, 22*. Should I throw it all away? Or leave it there? Yes, there was no other way for me. I could take only a minimum, only the bare essentials.

Then there was my stamp collection. In ten years of serious stamp collecting my collection had gained some unique specimens as well as complete runs. There were six albums with thousands of stamps in the permanent collection and in the album of exchanges. I simply had to take at least the most valuable ones in a small envelope, say a hundred of those I most valued.

On the bottom of my suitcase lay the icon, wrapped in a cloth. Then came some clothes, then the stamps, then the camera and some spare lenses. I put my personal documents in my briefcase, and threw various toiletries in a shoulder bag. That was it. My packing was done.

It was already light outside, but I had a few steps to go: to my two banks to withdraw some cash, to the travel agency to buy a ticket to Berlin, and of course to the Chinese restaurant for spring rolls. I always kept a fairly large sum of money at home — five or six thousand Marks, a few thousand Austrian shillings, and a wad of dollars. You never knew what unforeseen expenses there might be.

After taking some precautions I opened the door, went out, and took the main elevator down to the ground floor. The Arabella house was, as I have said, not just a huge building in which you could rent an apartment, but also a smart hotel with restaurants, shops, bars, and a swimming pool. There was something going on almost around the clock. I bought the newspapers, drank a coffee in a bar, and went for a walk around the building. It seemed as though nobody was following me. I noticed nothing suspicious. So I took a taxi and set off for the bank to withdraw money from my account.

I took a different taxi on my way back, stopped at my other bank, which was located in Arabella house, and cleared the account I had there. Then I bought a ticket for the afternoon flight to West Berlin from a travel agent. When the girl at the travel agency asked my name, I mumbled something vague so that the ticket bore a name nothing like Tumanov — I think it was something like Kumpana.

I decided not to tempt fate and used the same tried route for my departure. Although the words "they are all waiting for you" indicated that the KGB was ready to meet me at any of the previously agreed-on routes, of which there were several, the Berlin route seemed to me preferable because I would not have to show my passport when crossing the border. That meant that the risk of attracting attention was minimal. Of course, even there I could have problems.

Plane ticket in hand, I went to the Chinese restaurant, picked up my rolls, bought a bottle of vin rosé, and then returned home. It was only a few hours to takeoff. I had to take my leave. I wandered around the apartment, feeling the backs of my favorite books and the frames of my pictures, and drank the wine.

More than twenty years had passed since the day when I had jumped ship under cover of darkness, and began a journey with no foreseeable end. The journey could have ended on the beach if the Egyptians had caught me, or, shortly thereafter, if the Libyans had handed me over to the Soviet embassy. The Americans in the military intelligence in Frankfurt believed me, but it could have been the other way around. I had not had any special education, nor did I have any particular talents, but fate continued to smile on me — I was taken on by Radio Liberty and made myself a good career there. I was surrounded by beautiful furniture and with valuable paintings on the walls. My monthly salary was as much as the general secretary of the CPSU.

As a matter of fact the main part of my conscious life had been spent in Munich, and, after all, it had not all been taken up with spying. It was even difficult to say what had been most important—if that could ever be measured—the normal, decent life of a very prosperous citizen and émigré, or the illegal work of a KGB agent? Everything was interwoven, mixed up and united into one.

I long ago ceased to be afraid of being exposed. I no longer looked over my shoulder to see if I was being followed. It didn't bother me that my telephone was bugged. I no longer suspected friends and acquaintances of having been especially recruited to keep an eye on me. It couldn't have been otherwise. If it is true that all senses become duller with the passage of time, the sense of danger is no exception. Even at the front, soldiers soon lose their fear of bullets—if, of course, they remain alive. It seemed to me that "my" bullets had missed a long time ago. I was wrong—someone had at last gotten me in his sights.

It was time to go.

Suddenly, I caught myself thinking that I had never seriously considered returning to Moscow; that is to say, it had always been taken for granted but had seemed to be something very far away.

I went out into the hallway, picked up my modest luggage, and opened the door. I smiled involuntarily when it occurred to me that this was the door to an utterly different world—to the world in which I now had to spend the rest of my life. But I had no doubts about whether to cross the threshold.

Everything was the same at the airport. There was nothing suspicious. I checked in calmly, handed in my luggage, and sat down in a quiet corner of the bar, out of sight of passersby. I had to watch out, not just for police, but also for people I knew. I could do without their questions: Where are you off to, Oleg? Unlike previous trips to Berlin, this time I was much more vulnerable to suspicion. Nobody carried such a quantity of hard cash with him, and if they looked into my baggage and saw the postage stamps or the icon—I had far too many personal things. My flight was announced, but I was in no hurry to leave my hiding place. I was the last one to board the plane. They immediately shut the doors and within a few minutes we were taxiing for takeoff. I closed my eyes.

I reviewed what I had done that day in my mind. Had I done all I had to? Had I made any mistakes? I went back to the moment when the phone rang and the cheerful voice had told me of impending danger. I had acted without fuss or panic. I had not lost my head. I could swear I was not being followed. They had not caught me curled up in bed. They were now left with only one good means for catching me—closing the tunnel that went from West to East Berlin. That was their last opportunity. We would see.

No one at the radio station would miss me until the next day, when they discovered that I had not come to work. But not immediately; there were plenty of things the editor of the Russian service had to do in the morning.

I was absolutely calm when I arrived at Tempelhof Airport. I gained confidence from the fact that from here on I was almost certainly being watched by my own people. After all, the cheerful voice on the phone had told me that "they are all waiting for you." That meant that they were waiting and ready to meet me on this Berlin route.

Evening was approaching. The stream of Berliners hurrying through the border crossing had probably dried up. My lonely figure in the gloomy tunnel beneath Friedrichstrasse might attract attention. That meant I must wait, and spend one more night in the West. Leaving my belongings in a luggage locker at the airport, I went to a nearby hotel where I knew they wouldn't ask to see my documents or bother me with offers of girls or drinks. I ate all the Chinese rolls, watched the television for a while, and then went to sleep. When I awoke in the morning I was full of life, ready for any surprises.

On February 25, I—a well-dressed gentleman with a bag hanging from his shoulder and a case in his left hand—stepped out of the little hotel near the Friedrichstrasse. At the first crossroad I bought a bouquet of carnations. Then I headed for the underground border crossing. I now looked like a typical West German going to visit his poor relatives on the other side of the Berlin wall. Nobody paid me the slightest attention. I went down into the tunnel and walked almost to the point where East German border guards were checking documents. At that point, however, between the two worlds, I stopped walking with the other equally respectable looking gentlemen and stood by a scarcely noticeable door in the wall. I pressed the bell. The door opened. I was literally dragged inside. The door slammed shut.

There was now no way back for me. As I stepped across the threshold, I was immediately embraced by colleagues who had been waiting for me since the previous day.

As it turned out, KGB people had been watching me from the moment I left Tempelhof Airport. They had seen me collect my baggage and deposit it in the luggage locker. They had followed me almost to the hotel. But then they had lost me. It happened when I decided, just in case, to wander around the back streets near the hotel. I had wanted to shake off the enemy, but had succeeded instead in worrying my own people. Because of me they had lost a night's sleep, wondering where I was. I even think it possible that someone had decided that at the last minute I had changed my mind about returning home and had preferred to stay in the West. None of the illegal spies was completely trusted. I had deprived them of their sleep, while I had a wonderful rest.

Zhenya—the officer with whom I had gotten into such difficulties over my injured leg—was among the people who met me in the underground room. Others were phoning people and reporting something in excited voices. We soon went up to the surface, got into a blue Zhigulev and, accompanied by two other cars, set off for Karlshorst.

There, in a small office, a table had been laid for a standing reception—sandwiches, beer, and vodka. But nobody was touching the snacks; they were waiting for someone. The men who arrived with us were the same group that had followed me from Tempelhof. Zhenya asked how he could collect the rest of my baggage, and I gave him the locker number and key. No one else asked any questions.

The man the group had been waiting for soon arrived and introduced himself as Max. He invited everyone to help themselves to the refreshments. Zhenya then went off to pick up my luggage, the others departed, and Max and I were left alone. By evening the stamps, icon, ties, and other scraps of my life in the West were in East Berlin.

I knew (and still know) nothing about Max. He was apparently only superficially informed about me. He proposed: "Let's go to your new home. It's a villa not far from here and it's completely at your disposal. In a few days people will come from Moscow." We got into his Volga, drove a short way inside Karlshorst, and quickly found ourselves in a specially controlled zone with several large detached houses. From the outside, my new home did not create a good impression. Once inside, however, I immediately appreciated how comfortable it was. It had a large sitting room, an entrance hall, a kitchen, and an enclosed terrace downstairs, and three bedrooms with bathrooms upstairs. In addition, it came with a cheerful, skilled housekeeper named Galya who was ready to receive us with a richly prepared table.

At that time an antialcohol campaign was gathering strength in the Soviet Union and, as I later surmised, nobody would have risked consuming vodka and wine in the middle of the day. The party committees were on the alert and the most severe punishments were meted out for such offenses. But here, the rules were apparently different. The campaign against alcohol was eagerly discussed to the accompaniment of a glass of "Moscow" vodka.

Soon Zhenya arrived with my luggage. The guests took their leave, the housekeeper went off to wash the dishes, and I decided to get to know the house better. I immediately found a "toy" to play with—a new Sony video recorder and a pile of cassettes of Soviet films. They offered an excellent opportunity to pass the time and to familiarize myself with a way of life that I had partly forgotten.

That was the beginning of a period of stagnation in my life. When I awoke in the morning, I would drink a cup of coffee and glance through the morning papers. Then a young man who had come down specially from Moscow would question me until lunchtime. As far as I could make out, the young man was preparing to take over from Sergei or was being trained for illegal work in the West. He knew a lot about Radio Liberty and the emigration, but he wanted to know more and for that reason tortured me with his questions. In the evenings Galya would join me at the television. We would watch the news from Moscow and then switch on the video. Throughout that period I was not allowed to leave the house.

The stagnant period ended in the middle of March, when Max reappeared at the villa, this time with a smiling Sergei. He was the only one of all the people around me who knew the whole truth about everything that had happened to me. I was very glad to see him, since it meant that some change would soon take place in my monotonous way of life. And that was it: immediately after the cordial greetings and congratulations on the successful completion of a tremendous task, Sergei announced that I would soon return to Moscow. Everything was in order there and I had been allotted a temporary apartment. My brother did not know that I had left Radio Liberty, but all was well with him—Sergei had visited him before leaving Moscow.

"Here's a present for you," Sergei handed me a thin file of newspaper clippings. "You will learn a lot of interesting things about yourself."

The clippings contained various versions of my sudden disappearance as reported in the Western press. It appeared that the KGB could not resist the pleasure of continuing to play on the nerves of its enemies. I had been specially hidden away in a secret villa in Karlshorst and forbidden to leave it to prevent leaks about my fate. At the same time they observed the reaction of the special services and the media.

I greedily lost myself in the clippings. I was pleased to see that the majority of the newspaper reports cast no doubt on my loyalty to the West. On the contrary, they stressed my anti-Communist attitudes, my high standing at Radio Liberty, and my devotion to Western values. Journalists noted that in in my absence the Soviet Union had condemned me to death as a deserter. People constructed various, and sometimes highly fantastic, suggestions about what had happened to me. I cannot resist the pleasure of quoting some of them.

The International Herald Tribune: "Victor Gregory, deputy director of Radio Liberty and a friend of the missing editor, says he is shocked by the news of Tumanov's disappearance. According to him Oleg was a very well-balanced person who kept out of the bitter quarrels that have beset the radio station. Other colleagues valued highly his professional work as an editor."

Der Tagespiegel: "Tumanov's girlfriend could not offer the police any explanation about the circumstances of his disappearance. According to her, a stamp collection and a valuable icon were missing from Tumanov's apartment. It is possible that he has gone to Vienna or Stockholm to exchange or sell the stamps . . . "

New York Daily News: "Oleg Tumanov, chief editor of one of the departments of Radio Liberty, which operates under the direction of the United States, and a convinced anti-Communist, disappeared in Munich last week. His friends expect his body to be found and for it to be established that he was killed by agents of the KGB. Meanwhile his enemies believe the reverse—that he will appear at a press conference in Moscow as himself a KGB man.

"The forty-two-year-old Tumanov, who looks like a 'woolly bear,' twenty-one years ago jumped from a Soviet warship in the Mediterranean and swam six miles to escape from communism. For the last twenty years he has been working in the Munich headquarters of Radio Liberty and rose to a position permitting him to check and broadcast all the Russian-language programs.

"His friends said that he was ruined, had got into debt, had been drinking and was disappointed in love. . . . Other colleagues voiced the suggestion that he was a secret Soviet agent."

Novoye husskoye Slovo: "In 1966, Tumanov, who was then twenty-one, escaped from a Soviet submarine on which he served as a radio officer, and declared himself to be a defector . . . . Having been informed of Tumanov's disappearance, the West German police entered his apartment which had been left in great disorder by its occupant. Tumanov took everything of value and some documents with him. He had withdrawn his savings from his bank account the previous week. It is assumed that Oleg Tumanov has returned to the Soviet Union, although it is also possible that he has been kidnapped by the KGB."

The Arab Times (Kuwait): "According to sources in West Germany, the deputy chief editor of the Russian Service of Radio Liberty, Oleg Tumanov, has been drowned in one of the lakes near Munich."

In short, the journalists wrote as they pleased. In the beginning, the story circulating around the world, with quotes from my friends — suggested that I had simply dropped everything and gone off for a vacation in Italy. Then came the rumor about debts and an unhappy love affair. There were a great many different theories, often mutually exclusive. Victim of the KGB or a Moscow spy? My former bosses in Liberty insisted that "Tumanov appeared to be an irreconcilable anti-Communist and a convinced supporter of the West" and allegedly that all my efforts had been directed toward fighting the Soviet regime. Of course, in asserting this officials of Radio Liberty were primarily thinking about their reputation, not mine. After all, it was they who had promoted me to top jobs and had assisted in my career.

They were confronted by another version, spread mainly by representatives of the new Jewish emigration who insisted that I had been specially infiltrated into Radio Liberty/Radio Free Europe as a KGB agent to collect information and carrying out subversive acts. According to them I had caused a split between the Jews and the émigrés of other nationalities. They said I persecuted the Zionists and encouraged the broadcast of programs with an anti-Semitic bent. That was, of course, a lie. But they have to be given their due for having correctly forecast that in the near future I would turn up in Moscow, where I would appear at a press conference aimed at discrediting Radio Liberty/Radio Free Europe and the CIA. My former colleagues proved to be right.

With Sergei's arrival my compulsory imprisonment in the villa was partly cancelled. Accompanied by Zhenya and Galia I could now walk down the streets of Greater Berlin. From time to time we would visit bookshops, philatelists' businesses, and I had an opportunity to complete my wardrobe. This continued until the beginning of April.

Then one day Galia announced that I should expect a big shot from Moscow the next morning, and immediately began cleaning, vacuuming, and washing the already well cared for premises. Indeed, everything indicated that we were expecting a very big shot. Zhenya did not appear that day, and the phone didn't ring. So there was no way to get more details. I couldn't decide what to wear for the meeting. Should I put on a respectable suit and a tie or should I dress more informally? Galia insisted on the suit.

The next morning, at exactly nine o'clock, the doorbell rang. Galia quickly put on a raincoat, opened the door, and went out "on business." Max and an elderly, important-looking man, to whom I mentally gave the name "Grandpa," then appeared. Later I was told that "Grandpa" was a general, deputy to Vladimir Kryuchkov, head of the KGB's foreign-intelligence service. But I never learned his name. I don't know how it is now, but in those days I was rarely told the names of people in the secret departments. That was one of the unalterable rules of intelligence work. To inquire the name of a colleague or, more important, details of his biography, was unthinkable.

Despite his important appearance (you could tell he was a big shot), the suit "Grandpa" wore was unimpressive—in fact, his short brown cotton socks didn't even match. Involuntarily I hid my feet, with their expensive shoes and socks, under the table. Who could say: perhaps it was now considered improper to dress well in the KGB? But Max was dressed no worse than I.

"Grandpa" announced his desire to look over the villa. After discovering in the kitchen an impressive display of empty bottles that had contained strong drink, he muttered disapprovingly: "In Moscow we are waging a serious campaign against this." He was satisfied with the cleanliness and tidiness of the house, but annoyed that only coffee, and not tea, had been prepared for his arrival. The conversation that followed took no more than fifteen minutes.

"So here you are, Oleg Alexandrovich, you have been living here in Berlin, you've had a good rest and you have helped our people. You have really put your 'friends' in Munich in a difficult position: they don't know where to look for you, which embassies to apply to. Although I have to say that the brainier ones have already guessed where you are. So it is probably time for you to go home, isn't it? What do you think of that?"

The question was, of course, purely rhetorical. I had long wanted to get to Moscow—the period of stagnation was obviously being drawn out and was getting me down.

"Incidentally, we have already arranged an apartment for you in Moscow. It's an official one for the time being. Live in it for a while and settle down, then you can move into your own apartment. So, if you have no objection, I would like you to be ready to leave at seven o'clock tomorrow morning."

I escorted the visitors to the gate and waited until the two Volgas disappeared around the corner. Galia returned soon after and complained at the suddenness of my departure—so unexpected, so little time to tidy up. Not so unexpected, I thought. It had taken more than twenty years for me to find my way home. As the thoughtful Galia helped me to pack for the journey, she slipped a few bottles of brandy and a couple of packs of cigarettes from the villa's reserves (kept for show) into my case.

I tried to protest, but the housekeeper pointed out quite reasonably: "Have you forgotten about the antialcohol campaign? In Moscow you probably won't be able to buy anything stronger than lemonade. Our leaders have quite lost their heads." The future showed that she was right.

Back in Moscow

There was no band and no flowers. Nobody met me at the international airport, Sheremetyevo-2, when our plane arrived from East Berlin. No one but the dozen or so people from the KGB knew that secret agent Oleg Tumanov had completed his twenty-year assignment in the West and was returning home.

My return was surrounded in secrecy—as though in a short time I would have to go back again. At the Schoenefeld Airport, "Grandpa" and I were already in our seats in the first-class cabin of the Aeroflot plane when other passengers boarded. Our seats were then shut off from the rest of the plane with a thick curtain. An employee of the Berlin office of Aeroflot naïvely asked my companion to which organization our baggage should be addressed. "Grandpa" gave the man such a look that there were no further questions from the poor fellow. "Do as you please," he growled.

"Grandpa" was obviously not in good spirits. Later I learned why: the general didn't like flying. A few glasses of brandy during the flight made him more agreeable.

In Moscow we were the last to leave the plane. After the bus with the other passengers had driven away, an officer of the border troops took us to a grey official Volga waiting on the tarmac. The general got into the front seat and off we went.

I was home. Not for a short stay, not as a foreign guest, as a citizen—a Muscovite. Why was I not overflowing with feelings of exaltation? Perhaps because the game was still going on and I could not yet behave like a normal Soviet citizen. I was taken to a KGB official apartment which, "Grandpa" instructed me, I was not to leave for the time being. I was to have a twenty-four-hour guard which would not only be responsible for my physical security but would also record my telephone calls. I could not yet see even my brother.

I was home, but I was no longer the Oleg Tumanov who had left the country in 1965 in a sailor's uniform. It was as though I had led two separate lives, and was about to begin a third. What would it be like? What would it bring me? For the moment only one thing was clear: the intelligence people would allow me to live only according to their strict rules.

We arrived in one of Moscow's new districts—an area of totally identical multistory buildings. I had never been there before. Everything gave me the feeling that this gigantic, featureless "bedroom" had only recently been occupied, that the people were all recent arrivals, and that they were looking around at themselves in surprise. My new temporary abode was a pleasant three-room apartment with the requisite housekeeper, called Tamara, and a young man named Gena, who was responsible for internal protection. Gena was apparently being trained for a long period of work abroad in some *rezidentura*, because he spent hours extracting from me the smallest details of life in the West. Apart from that there was also an outside guard—two cars, each with three men, stood at the corner of the building twenty-four hours a day. Actually they preferred to be in the special-duty room in the basement watching everyone who approached the entrance. The guard was changed every eight hours.

It is difficult for me to say to what extent such security measures were justified. My former colleagues in Munich or Frankfurt were hardly likely to try to get me back. But who knows? The history of the special services contains some apparently incredible episodes. The "Chekists" have kidnapped people they wanted on the territory of West Germany, France, and other countries. It is also common knowledge that British intelligence and the CIA worked out a plan to seize and secretly remove a member of the famous "Cambridge Five," Donald Maclean, from Moscow. Maclean had worked for the KGB for many years. He managed to slip out of the Soviet Union on the eve of his arrest, even though the British had gone as far as to involve specialists in the analysis of information received from satellites—asking them to study photographs of the Moscow district where Maclean lived taken from a great height—to ensure that he was captured. That episode was recalled in the Western biographies of the "Cambridge spies," by Kim Philby, who lived in Moscow for twenty-five years after his escape from Beirut, and was obliged to have an officer next to him who was responsible for his safety until his death.

Although the table in the apartment was already set with refreshments, "Grandpa" asked us to refrain from eating. He left immediately, and in his place a brigade of six doctors, with all sorts of medical apparatus, arrived.

"Don't worry," the eldest doctor reassured me. "We have to draw up a general medical map of your state of health."

One of the rooms was turned into a sick room. I weakly objected, but they were not particularly interested in whether I wanted to go through the examination. They just told me what to do. An hour later the whole brigade, having refused to take refreshment and apparently quite content, departed.

The officer who accompanied us from the airport pointed to the well-loaded table and amazed me with an unexpected statement. "You will notice, Oleg Alexandrovich," he said sternly, "that there are no strong drinks. From now on we drink only beer and mineral water. It's all over with vodka."

Oh well, I thought to myself, we shall see how long you will find that enough. I had no intention of changing my habits, as I informed my new acquaintance straight out.

In the first few days of my life in Moscow, "Grandpa" and some other higher-ups announced that I was to appear at a press conference at the press center of the Ministry of Foreign Affairs.

"You will tell the Soviet and foreign journalists what exactly radio station Liberty is. How closely it is linked with the special services of the United States. How it continues to wage the Cold War. You will name the people and the jobs they do. It will be a sensation."

A sensation? Frankly, the idea did not evoke the slightest enthusiasm in me. It was one thing to be a secret agent sending back information about people regarded as enemies of your country, but it was something quite different to make speeches in public. I realized that the journalists, especially those from the West, would not believe a single word I spoke and would demand proof. I had never felt confident when facing a large audience, and I had no experience in public speaking. This press conference threatened to turn into a painful squabble. But it was something else that finally finished me off.

The details of the forthcoming press show had been agreed to, I gathered, "at the very top"—in other words, by the highest party and state leaders. As the KGB saw it, I was to appear before the journalists in my true character—as a spy. But someone unexpectedly interfered with the plan—Andrei Gromyko, the man who formally occupied the highest position in the state as chairman of the Presidium of the Supreme Soviet of the USSR. Gromyko is mainly remembered as the foreign minister to whom the Western press, with good reason, gave the name "Mister No." After studying the Lubyanka's plan for the press conference he flatly opposed my appearance as a spy.

"We don't spy," he told a high official of the KGB, "and never have." There was no sense in disagreeing.

It did not pay to contest the views of people at Gromyko's level, whatever nonsense they talked. Of course the former foreign minister knew no less (and probably more) than other people about the scale of the Soviet Union's intelligence activities. For many years running, an intelligence summary and reports from some of the especially important agents—drawn up in the First Chief Directorate of the KGB—had been placed on his desk each morning. He was personally acquainted with many of the generals in Yasenevo, where the headquarters of the First Directorate was situated, and was on friendly terms with some of them. "We don't have spies" was not a joke or an old man's whim but one of the rules of the top officials' mentality that had been established under Stalin. The existence and activities of external espionage, which was a fact widely discussed throughout the world, still remained a secret hidden from the Soviet people.

My superiors feverishly began to rewrite the scenario. In the end I had to appear before the public as a fugitive sailor who had been caught in the skillfully set nets of the CIA, who now had seen the error of his ways and returned to his country in the spirit of repentance. The story gave off a bad smell. That such a story was quite unconvincing could be seen a mile away. The people who had to take me through the new "legend" felt the same—I saw how awkward they felt. But I didn't have strength enough to refuse to go through with this thankless role in a doubtful spectacle. They drew up a lengthy statement that I was to read at the beginning of the press conference and we rehearsed possible replies to tricky questions from correspondents. The press department of the foreign ministry was instructed to inform the press and prepare the hall. It seemed as though no surprises were expected from any direction.

But, as often happens, a blow came from the most unexpected direction. A few days before the press conference, I awoke during the night with a sharp pain in my lower back. I felt sick. Then came other symptoms that I recognized from earlier attacks in Germany. I had kidney stones. Anyone who has experienced this will understand me. I would have to lie in a hot bath, take a strong diuretic every twenty or thirty minutes and drink mineral water mixed with milk. And it did no harm to take a painkiller.

I woke Tamara and explained the situation to her. The bath, the milk, the mineral water, and the painkiller were all available. But the most important medicine—the strong diuretic—was not. When Gena awoke he called the doctor. By then the pain had become sharper and, in an effort to reduce it, I had gulped down half a glass of the brandy (from my Berlin reserves), and started walking around the room. The attack became so painful that I lost consciousness and collapsed. It was as well that Gena was next to me because he quickly brought me around. Everything would have been fine if I had not hit the floor with the left side of my face when I fell. The doctors arrived shortly thereafter and were amazed at what they saw. They had been summoned to treat an attack of kidney stones, yet they were presented with a man with a serious bruise under his left eye.

Once things were sorted out, the doctors set about dealing with my kidneys. By midday the stones had been removed. Despite all medical efforts, the bruise was getting worse — taking on some very bright colors. By the next morning it was absolutely clear that I could not appear at a press conference.

Perhaps fate itself was offering me a delay?

I recalled some Western newspaper reports that I had been kidnapped by the KGB and that I was being forced by torture to fling mud at the West. My bruise would serve as graphic illustration of how the "brutes in the Lubyanka" operated.

In the evening a meeting of worried bosses took place in the apartment. They debated what to do. A KGB enterprise — agreed upon and confirmed at the very top, that promised its initiators, they believed, an obvious success — was now threatened. Tamara shyly offered the guests coffee. As the sufferer, I brazenly drank Greek brandy. I offered some to the others, but they waved it away. They didn't want it. Of course they *did* want it, but their fear of each other was stronger than their desire for the brandy. The famous antialcohol campaign was then gathering strength and more than one official had been deprived of his party membership, which meant losing his job as well, because of a passion for spirits.

It was "Grandpa," who arrived later, who found a way to take the heat out of the difficult situation. First he bravely drank a glass of brandy with me, and then he asked that a video recorder, and as many cassettes as possible, be brought to the apartment. After that, the bosses, now a little calmer, set about discussing the main problem. In the end, the press conference was postponed for two weeks and I was subjected to intensive treatment until the bruise had completely disappeared.

"Confined to bed!" Grandpa ordered. "Lie still and watch films. No sudden body movements!"

"Don't you worry," I said in a conciliatory tone, "a shell never falls in the same hole twice."

On April 26, having been twice examined by the doctors and now declared to be absolutely fit, I was again involved in work. I was driven to Zubov Square, the location of the foreign ministry's press center.

The impressive hall had booths for the simultaneous translators, fixed television cameras, an auditorium with arm chairs, and a big platform. It all depressed me. I felt very acutely how uncomfortable I was going to be on that stage, in sight of everybody, and I was even less pleased to see the deputy head of the press center, Yuri Gremitskikh. With scarcely a nod to the "fugitive sailor," he spoke to me in a very condescending tone—one that conveyed snobbery and arrogance. It was alarming to think that this man was entrusted with the task of chief producer of the approaching spectacle, and that the success of the show depended on his intelligence, professionalism, and tact. The two of us were to appear on the stage together—he as the man in charge of the press conference, and I as its main participant. I already knew that we would not produce a harmonious duet.

A Flop by the Kremlin

On April 28, the hall of the foreign ministry press center was packed. Journalists squeezed into the doors and stood in the aisles. They were expecting a sensation. In the end there were three of us on the stage: myself, Gremitskikh, and an international lawyer tasked with demonstrating that the very existence of Radio Liberty was illegal from the point of view of international law.

A sigh of disappointment went around the hall when Yuri Gremitskikh introduced me:

"Today you will be addressed by the Soviet citizen Tumanov who has lived for a long time in the West. While abroad he was drawn into anti-Soviet activity by the special services of the USA. From 1966 Tumanov worked in one of the main centers of the West's ideological subversion, the radio station Liberty. In recent years Tumanov occupied a leading position as chief editor of the Russian service and by the nature of his work was well informed and had access to secret information. In the course of his work, he became convinced of the subversive activity of the organization, which was profoundly hostile to the Soviet people, and, realizing his mistake, returned to his own country."

This was all said in the second year of *Perestroika*, when Gorbachev was assuring people everywhere of the sincerity and openness of new Soviet policy. It was difficult to imagine a more uninspired or unprofessional speech. I was sitting next to him, suffering. Why on earth was it necessary to make a clown of me? "Drawn by the special services of the USA . . . realizing his mistake . . . " I was a spy who had carried out assignments from the secret department. I had nothing to be ashamed of. I hadn't murdered anybody, hadn't stolen any documents, and hadn't organized any subversive activities. As far as was in my power, I had warned Moscow of any hostile moves being planned against the Soviet Union. I can tell about it here: What was there to conceal? Why were they still using the absurd, official Stalinist rhetoric?

When Gremitskikh finished, I read the official "Statement by Oleg Tumanov." I had, of course, had a very small part in writing the document. I will quote it here, with some cuts, as a typical example of the KGB's official "creative work":

"Comrades, ladies and gentlemen!

"I must begin by explaining why I am here today, in the press center of the foreign ministry of the USSR, and not in my office in the headquarters of Radio Liberty and Radio Free Europe on No. 67 Oetingerstrasse in Munich.

"I have to begin a long way back.

"At the end of November 1965, a sailor, Oleg Tumanov, born in Moscow in 1944, disappeared from a Soviet warship lying in the Mediterranean. For some time my disappearance was regarded as an accident, but it was actually an escape.

"The British and American intelligence services decided fairly quickly who should have me, and in the first days of December 1965 a United States Air Force plane took me to Frankfurt-on-Main in West Germany. I ended up in the famous Camp King—a system of camps for training and screening displaced persons and émigrés from Eastern European countries and the Soviet Union. The affairs of Camp King were directed by military intelligence and the CIA of the United States.

"I foresee a question that I will answer right away. What actually made me escape and commit treachery?

"That difficult question has been put to me dozens of times. I can only say that I was then only about twenty years old, that I wanted to take my fate into my own hands, that there was an element of egotism in it, as well as ignorance of the consequences. Everything played its part. I had no problems on the ship. My service was coming to an end, my father and mother were waiting for me in Moscow. I repeat once more that it is very, very difficult to answer the question of why I deserted. I have already said that there was the hope of taking my fate into my own hands. Unfortunately, things turned out differently. I fell into the hands of American intelligence.

"In the camp I was dealt with by a colonel of the CIA, Alex Limbarsky, also known as Lane, Logan, and Pavlo. Colonel Limbarsky is now retired, but he continues to be involved in the work to which he is accustomed — the collection of information about the USSR and the countries of Eastern Europe.

"I spent six months in Camp King, where I went through every possible kind of screening and rescreening. Because of some of the questions I was asked, I believe that the American embassy in Moscow played some part in my screening. I was also put through a lie detector test.

"Sometime in February or March 1966, Colonel Limbarsky brought two employees of Radio Liberty who worked 'in a special department dealing with the assessment of the effectiveness of Liberty's broadcasts in influencing Soviet listeners' to meet me. One was George Perry, an American diplomat or, more precisely, spy, who had been expelled from the USSR. The other was Edward Neimanis, also an employee of American intelligence. After a few talks and meetings I was invited to visit Radio Liberty.

"That was in 1966. At that time the employees of the radio station consisted mainly of former war criminals, people who had fought in Vlasov's army, displaced persons, and representatives of the White Guard emigration. It was clear that, with such a staff, it would not take long to lose the last few listeners, and that there was an urgent need for 'new blood.' I was invited to work at the station, despite my lack of any special training for or experience in radio.

"I now want to say a few words about what exactly Radio Liberty is. Senator Fulbright called it, and the radio station Free Europe, relics of the Cold War. The senator probably hoped that the international climate would get warmer and thought the relics would disappear of their own accord.

"But ten years have passed and the two radio stations continue to exist in their previous form, as 'dogs of the Cold War.'

"Radio Liberty and Radio Free Europe are branches of American intelligence services, a convenient screen behind which operations against the Soviet Union and other Socialist countries can be carried out. The visible part of the iceberg, the so-called propaganda activity aimed at introducing into the minds of Soviet citizens ideas that suit the special services, is very limited. The invisible part, which the widespread audience does not know about but which is the most important part of the radio station's work, is involved in spying. This is, incidentally, no secret to the government of West Germany. At one time the

Social–Democratic government suggested to the Americans that they should remove the radio stations from the territory of West Germany but, as you see, this did not happen, and it is possible that one of the reasons for this is the close relations between the CIA and the West German intelligence service.

"Over the course of my years working at the radio station, I read many documents, attended conferences with leading officials, and spoke personally with representatives of the special services of the United States. I can say with confidence, therefore, that the people in charge of every section of the radio station include employees of the CIA and military intelligence.

"Through the mediation of the CIA, the American embassy in Moscow also helps Radio Liberty. It informs Radio Liberty about the quality of programs directed to the Soviet Union, their effectiveness, and how well they are received. All information from Moscow passes through the United States consulate-general in Munich, which has a special department for contact with the radio station.

"I think I have indicated, with sufficient clarity, the role played by the radio station in the intelligence system. As you know, such activity requires considerable financial investment. In terms of the rate of growth in its budget, Radio Liberty is one of the first places after the Pentagon and the CIA. And that is in spite of the fact that the Reagan administration has recently been trying to reduce expenditures on civil servants. The American taxpayer will surely be interested in the salaries paid to Radio Liberty employees. The most important employees receive a salary equal to that of a Congressman, plus all sorts of privileges, including free accommodations and a car; they are much better off than employees of the Voice of America, which is a federal radio station!

"I have lived in the West for more than twenty years. I have lived through periods of tension and of détente. But the role and the tasks of Radio Liberty have never changed. Whatever the international climate, Radio Liberty has remained the mouthpiece of the militant group of politicians for whom the very word détente is more frightening than a wasp's sting.

"The radio station was always hostile to the Soviet Union, but its present attitude is something special. It repeats the policy line that the United States government has adopted toward the USSR exactly. It is a policy of sudden worsening of relations between the two states, of ignoring any peaceful initiatives made by the Soviet leadership, a policy aimed at increasing international tension.

"Radio Liberty likes to boast of its efficient operation — 'we broadcast this ten minutes sooner than the Voice of America and that twenty minutes before the *Deutsche Welle*.' Do you know how such efficiency is sometimes achieved?

"I used to keep in my safe a copy of an obituary notice for President Reagan. It was regularly updated after a new event in his life. When instructions are received, the obituary notice will be broadcast. There are similar notices for other public figures. Sometimes things go wrong. On one occasion President Carter's obituary was copied and distributed to the editors. One department didn't notice the word 'embargo,' with the result that President Carter's death was announced prematurely. Such material is no longer distributed but kept in a safe.

"In conclusion, I would like to say a few more words about myself. My journey home was not easy. I don't wish anybody to have to live through such a twenty-year experience. I am now home and it might seem that the simplest thing would be to say that everything I lived through was a bad dream. But no, it was not a dream. Everything that I have told you is true—a nightmarish reality. But not everybody will be able to assess that reality objectively. I succeeded in doing that, and my way home was therefore natural and logical."

Once I had read this absurd text, which prompted many of the correspondents to ask puzzled questions and others to laugh outright—I sat back in my chair with relief and took a sip of mineral water. For some reason I thought that now that I had explained the affair the newsmen would go away and that would be the end of it. That's not what happened. I must remind you that the whole business took place at the beginning of *glasnost*, when there was still a great shortage of interesting information in Moscow and, with rare exceptions, Soviet correspondents were still afraid of swimming against the tide, while the foreign newsmen felt they could do as they pleased. The foreigners, having decided that they had been led down the garden path once again, angrily directed questions at me.

I was naïve in thinking that we had rehearsed replies to all possible tricky questions and that I couldn't be caught off guard. The was not the case. Determined to get to the bottom of the affair, the correspondents began shooting caustic questions at me from all sides. Gremitskikh, who was running the conference, obviously lost his head and let things go their own way, as if to say: let the "fugitive sailor" get out of this mess himself.

All this provided *Time* magazine with grounds for saying: "The perspiring and mumbling Tumanov's story evoked disbelief and laughter among more than a hundred reporters invited to this well-rehearsed propaganda show. . . . " in its next issue.

The reports of some other Western correspondents were written in even stronger terms. The majority of Soviet newspapers, which were then still under the complete control of the Central Committee of the CPSU, published only the official *TASS* report of the press conference — ignoring the material sent in by their own correspondents.

The torture of the conference lasted three hours.

One well-informed journalist inquired: "Leaflets appeared periodically at the radio station with an obviously anti-Semitic 'pogrom' content. What is that? Is it also the result of your 'secret war'? Are you not known at Radio Liberty as an open anti-Semite?"

I replied weakly, "If you are informed in such detail about the situation at Radio Liberty, *you* should be able to tell everybody here who distributes those leaflets. As for me, I have never belonged to the anti-Semites. I had friends of various nationalities at the radio station, and my former wife was Jewish. If some employees of Radio Liberty were not satisfied with my work as an editor, let them look at their own faults. When a program is badly put together it remains bad whoever did it, a Jew, a Russian, or an Armenian. True, I must point out that there was always a higher percentage of bad programs written by Jews, but there was a simple reason for that: Jews were in the majority on the staff of the Russian service."

"Almost two months have passed since your disappearance from the radio station, Mr. Tumanov. Where have you been all that time? Have you not been subjected to the Soviet Union's ways of bringing pressure to bear like those which, according to statements by the Soviet authorities, were used by the Americans on Yurchenko?"

KGB Colonel Vitali Yurchenko had sat in the very same place the year before. He had also been the hero of a sensational press conference. Yurchenko had served in the directorate of foreign counterintelligence, and later in the American department of the First Directorate. In the summer of 1985, while on an official mission in Rome, he had disappeared without a trace. One month later the KGB discovered that the colonel was living quietly in a CIA villa near Washington and exposing KGB agents, one after the other, to the Americans. Incidentally, the directorate of foreign intelligence was also in charge of operational control of my affairs. It was my good fortune that internal discipline in that directorate was well organized because Yurchenko had never heard of me. It was later discovered that Yurchenko had "sold" the Americans a number of very important KGB operatives. But three months later he suddenly made the inexplicable decision to return to Moscow. He tricked the CIA bodyguard and turned up at the Soviet embassy, ready